The Christia

Rich Toward God

Ken Pearson

*But God said to him, 'You fool! This very night your life
will be demanded from you. Then who will get what you
have prepared for yourself?'*

*This is how it will be with anyone who stores up things
for himself but is not rich toward God*

Luke 12:20,21

Gen2Rev
PUBLISHING

First published in Great Britain in 2012

Gen2Rev Publishing
19 Hillside Road, Bath BA2 3NU
Email: ken.n.pearson@btinternet.com

First published 2012

ISBN:978-0-9574447-0-6

Produced on paper from sustainable forests.

Print management by www.printbridge.co.uk
Design by Melanie Dixey

Contents

Acknowledgments

This book has been a long time in the making. The original idea was born as a result of a sermon by the minister of my church in South Africa back in the early eighties. He called Joseph 'the first steward in the Bible'. That set me thinking. Joseph may have been the first person in the Bible to be called a steward but Adam was the first steward. And from that thought developed the basic theme of the book.

It was written because of a growing personal conviction about Christian giving and also about the great need for a renewal of giving (of all kinds) within the Church. The book is not, however, intended for any one church or denomination but for the whole Church, both corporately and as individual members of the body of Christ.

I owe a great debt to the late Dr Stephen Olford, whose ministry and 'grace of giving' has had a profound influence on my life. Then it was the late Roman Catholic Bishop of Johannesburg, Bishop Reginald Orsmond, who provided the opportunity to develop a programme of fundraising in his parishes - his faith in me was a great encouragement. The programme was based on one used by Pat Ryan of Staley, Robeson, Ryan and St Lawrence of Cincinnati, USA. I learnt a great deal on the modern practice of fundraising from the late Terry Murray and from Jenni McLeod of Downes, Murray International of Durban, South Africa; and from Michael Downes of Downes, Venn and Associates of Australia. I must also thank Everald Compton, an elder in the Uniting Church in Australia and founder of Everald Compton International of Brisbane, Australia; and author of *Where Have The Christian Stewards Gone?* Then I must thank Prebendary Richard Askew and the people of Bath Abbey for their love, support and willingness to try out some of the principles expounded in this book. Bath Abbey 2000 and The Luke 12: 34 Challenge are a testimony to their faithfulness. I am also grateful for the support and encouragement I have had from David

Saint, the chairman of Action Planning and an elder in the United Reform Church in the UK. I have been a Senior Consultant with Action Planning and have learnt a great deal from my colleagues.

My background is varied. I trained as a marine engineering technician but left engineering for a year at Rosebank Bible College in Johannesburg in 1975. Then followed twelve years split between Youth for Christ, Encounter Ministries SA, and The Leprosy Mission. I joined a fundraising consultancy in 1987 and ran a capital campaign for the Roman Catholic Schools in Soweto and then planned-giving campaigns for eleven Roman Catholic parish churches. I also helped a Methodist and a Presbyterian church with their planned-giving campaigns. Most of the experience was gained in South Africa but a move to England (I was born in Lancashire) in 1991 to be the campaign manager of a capital campaign for Bath Abbey (and later a planned giving campaign called The Luke 12: 34 Challenge) resulted in the book being written in England.

After twelve years in missionary work and then six with two international fundraising consultancies to learn more about the modern practice of fundraising, I am convinced that many of the principles used in fundraising in the 21st century are biblical principles.

My debt, as it has been for over forty years, is to the Word of God. It is a constant source of guidance and encouragement and my hope and prayer is that this is reflected in this book.

Writing a book takes time, especially when it must be done outside of working hours - hours that otherwise would have been spent with the family. So I dedicate this book to my wife, Rita, and my daughters, Jeanine, Louise and Christy. Their faith is a joy to me and I thank the Lord for His goodness to us all.

Foreword

It would be unusual to find the words 'theological', 'practical' and 'funding' in the same sentence, but these are the three key word that apply to this book – a practical, theologically-sound guide to funding Christian work – from the point of view of the giver as well as the asker.

But then the book's author is an unusual man. Ken Pearson has a long and distinguished career as a professional fundraiser for Christian causes. He is a man of deep personal faith, which has informed his choice of academic study – he holds a Bachelor of Theology degree, and a postgraduate degree in the Old Testament. Ken is now planning to bring together the professional, theological and academic strands of his life in a Master of Theology research degree, examining Anglican and Baptist fundraising in the UK.

Perhaps surprisingly, money is one of the most common themes in the Bible, and yet it is one of the most difficult topics for Christians to discuss. Christian givers may ask, "How much should I give?" "Should I tithe on my income before or after tax?" "Should I save for a rainy day, or does that show a lack of faith?" And Christian askers (churches, charities etc.) may ask "Is it fair to keep asking more of the same people?" "How can I broach the subject of legacies with my parishioners?" "What can we do to stop our income declining further?"

This uncompromising, wide-ranging and well-referenced book will provide many of the answers – some of them surprising. It is a truly refreshing look at issues that have faced Christians ever since the Apostle Paul encouraged some of the earliest fellowships to support their poorer brothers and sisters. And one of the things that make it refreshing is that in the one volume the author explores these issues from the point of view of both giver and the asker, which has the added benefit of enabling each to have a better understanding of the other's perspective.

Ken traces stewardship back to its original formulation in the relationship between God and Adam. And it is also a very modern concept as we become increasingly aware of the stewardship we have over the Earth and its resources, the stewardship in the national interest that has to be exercised by Governments, and the stewardship responsibilities of the people who run multinational corporations.

But the central premise of this book is that we are *all* stewards – stewards of what we have personally, and stewards of what we are given to work with if we have responsibility for a church, or a Christian charity. Whether you are the widow stewarding her 'mite', or the Fundraising Director of a major charity with a multi-million pound target, in this book you will find practical, theologically-sound inspiration to help you become "rich toward God".

I am delighted to commend it to you.

David Saint
Chairman, Action Planning
August 2012

Introduction

Possibly the most prophetic words about the Church in the western world in the post-Second World War period come in J B Phillips's dynamic translation of Romans 12: 2

> *Don't let the world around you squeeze you into its own mould ...* but let God remould your minds from within, so that you may prove in practice that the plan of God for you is good, meets all His demands and moves towards the goal of true maturity.

There is always the danger that Christians will take their lead from the world and be squeezed into its mould. This was the constant warning God gave through the Old Testament prophets. And the prophetic word in Jeremiah 6:13, 'From the least to the greatest, all are greedy for gain' is perhaps more true now than ever before.

And the Apostle Paul made it very clear to Timothy in his first letter:

> If anyone teaches false doctrines and does not agree to the sound instruction of our Lord Jesus Christ and to godly teaching, he is conceited and understands nothing. He has an unhealthy interest in controversies and arguments that result in envy, quarrelling, malicious talk, evil suspicions and constant friction between men of corrupt mind, who have been robbed of the truth and who think that *godliness is a means to financial gain.*
> *But godliness with contentment is great gain.* For we brought nothing into this world, and we can take nothing out of it. But if we have food and clothing, we will be content with that. People who want to get rich fall into temptation and a trap and into many foolish and harmful desires that plunge men into ruin and destruction. For the love of money is a root for all kinds of evil. Some people, eager for money, have wandered from the faith and pierced themselves with many griefs. **1 Timothy 6: 3 - 10**

Is your goal godliness or gain? If it is gain then you will never be content. But if you aim for godliness then with it comes great gain, both in this world and the next!

This world is taken up with the pursuit of getting as much as possible out of life - but does not seem to have the same concern over putting something back into it. The preoccupation with the pursuit of getting rather than giving is symptomatic of the age in which we live. In the UK this has followed the philosophy of government since the Second World War and has gone through three stages: the welfare state, the 'yuppie state', and the 'circus state'.

The welfare state was a grand design for life without need. The government undertook to care for its citizens from the cradle to the grave. Everyone was equal; everyone had the right to free education, free medical care and a state pension (of course these were never free but paid for by citizens through their taxes). The National Health Service gave free medical care to all citizens and even visitors could benefit from its largess. Utopia had arrived. Everyone was entitled to the benefits of the welfare state, regardless of their employment status. The system was meant to protect those who were without work and so they could claim additional benefits. The theory was wonderful. But a change in attitudes soon became apparent. Soon some people found that claiming their rights was preferable to working. Abuse of the system through fraudulent claims enables many to live, often very comfortably, without having to work. This ranks as one of the most lucrative forms of unorganised crime (and in many cases it is organised), costing the government (i.e. you and me) many billions every year.

The welfare state has seen a major swing in perception: citizens claim their rights but their responsibilities are largely overlooked. Because of its nature the welfare state has had a dramatic effect on philanthropy. The state assumed responsibility for education, health and pensions, which were paid for out of social security contributions, another form of taxation. In theory philanthropy is no longer needed in these areas - although there are always some people who fall through the net. People have directed their giving to new areas but they become accustomed to the idea of government support and so the state faced demands for aid from a variety of sources. Real philanthropy is eroded as the government pays for more and more.

The 'yuppie state', starting in the Thatcher era, was in one respect the pendulum swinging the other way. Some people didn't want to be equal. They wanted more, particularly if they had worked harder. It was their right, their reward for being industrious. Suddenly there were a lot of young people with a lot of money and a lifestyle to match their newfound wealth. Are they any more philanthropic because they have money to spend? Do they have anything of the old concept of noblesse oblige? Or do they consider the extra taxes they pay at the higher rate sufficient obligation? There are exceptions but generally such people see giving as a business transaction - how else would they view it? 'What is in it for them?' is often their question when it comes to their charitable giving. And charities have become obsessed with developing strategies that bring recognition to donors for their gifts. Millions of pounds are spent in trying to persuade people to be philanthropic! Company sponsorship, rather than grants, is now almost the norm for giving from the business sector and it has its equivalent in giving by individuals. Philanthropy suffers another blow.

The pendulum has swung from left to right but the government still cannot meet all the needs. It pays for the medical care that enables people to live longer but then finds it does not have the money to meet the pension bill. How will it make ends meet? It arranges for a circus to come to town. Not a free circus, for this is not ancient Rome, but a circus nevertheless. It is a very clever circus as it promises, for a very modest fee, to help *charity*, and more wonderful than ever, it has a multi-million-pound carrot to dangle before the eyes of the greedy. Because the lottery is now a major component in charity thinking there is more on it later in the book but suffice it to say that the lottery has moved Britain further away from philanthropy and highlighted the desire to get more rather than give more.

The argument is that the three 'states' have diminished the practice of philanthropy. Secularism and its natural partner, materialism, have worked through the system to establish the 'me' generation. The charity sector in the United Kingdom is concerned about these trends, as it gets more difficult and expensive to recruit volunteers and donors.

What about the corporate sector? Companies go to a lot of trouble and expense, often employing public relations consultants in an effort to try to prove they do have a social concern programme. Yet in Britain there are very few companies that give even as much as one per cent of their profits to charitable causes. There is a Per Cent Club of companies in the UK. They undertake to give at least one per cent of their pre-tax profits to charity. This need not be all in cash but includes gifts in kind and the secondment of staff. This was an increase in 2000 as previously it was only half of one per cent. And a method of checking was introduced. A survey by Business in the Community, which administers the Club, revealed that of the FTSE top fifty companies twenty-six gave less than one per cent of pre-tax profit. In America there is a similar organisation but its member companies give between *two and ten* per cent - many times the level of British companies.

This is the world's mould - a decline in giving, a decline in philanthropy. The Church must beware of falling into the same trap. For the fact is that Christians are primarily called to serve and you cannot serve without giving. This follows the very clear example of our Servant King,

> ... just as the Son of Man did not come to be served, but to serve, and to give his life as a ransom for many. **Matthew 20: 28**

Christianity is primarily a relationship and a relationship is a two-way street. We are not concerned only with receiving from God but also giving to him. Certainly, we receive all the benefits of our faith as gifts from a loving heavenly Father. The Father has sent his Son and his Spirit to be his gifts for our salvation and sanctification. The gift of salvation and the gifts of the Spirit are the evidence of our Father's goodness.

Can we ever repay him? No, obviously not.

Does he expect anything in return? Yes, everything we are and have belongs to him.

When Pope John Paul II visited America it was reported that Frank Sinatra was prepared to give a huge sum, hundreds of millions of dollars, to the Catholic Church for an audience with the Pope. The sum was reputed to be half of all that Sinatra possessed. Sinatra had his own reasons for wanting an audience, but if he thought he could buy his way into heaven he was mistaken. Getting into heaven costs nothing and everything. It costs nothing as the price has already been paid at Calvary. But if he wanted to make an offering to the Lord then he was 50 per cent short. He did not get the audience with the Pope.

Sinatra once had a hit with a song called 'My Way'. From a biblical perspective this is probably one of the most unchristian titles in all the history of recorded music. For 'there is a way that seems right to a man, but in the end it leads to death' (Proverbs 14: 12). God wants us to follow His way. The Lord Jesus Christ made it perfectly clear, 'I am the way, the truth and the life. No one comes to the Father except through me' (John 14: 6). Sinatra's song epitomises the way of the sinner - doing his own thing, ignoring God and his ways. It is the basis of the selfish, materialistic culture of the West.

After Frank Sinatra died *The Daily Telegraph* of 16 May 1998 carried a resume of his life, including an article entitled, 'How My Way became the drunk's anthem'. To quote one paragraph:

The appeal of *My Way* lies in the way it offers not just absolution but glorification to the perpetrator of all the most

> dastardly deeds, reassuring the selfish that they are courageous
> and the thuggish that they are noble. It also lets the loser see
> himself as a winner. Had the song been around in 1945, one can
> be sure that Adolf Hitler, tears in his eyes, would have been
> warbling it in his bunker.

Materialism, the 'me first, my way' culture of the western world appears, at times, to have been adopted by the Church. Why do we hear so much about what we should be receiving from God and so little about what we should be giving to him?

The Lord Jesus had many profound things to say about money and told a striking parable about a rich fool, a man who had money and kept it to himself, and a man who was 'not rich toward God'. Have we forgotten, have we never been taught, that Christians can be rich towards our God?

At a time when people are wealthier and have more disposable income than ever before is this reflected in church giving? The shocking situation is that giving in the mainstream denominations is appalling. This appears to be a problem in most western countries, not just Britain. There are exceptions, but most people are too polite, or too embarrassed, to be honest about it.

Christians seldom talk openly about giving (see Chapter 10 on demythologising giving in the Church). A crisis is looming in many of the mainstream denominations because of falling income. It is a problem that many church leaders are ignoring or wishing would just go away. Prayer is called for and that spiritualises the condition but does not resolve the problem. Certainly prayer *is* needed. But when it is within our capacity to provide the answers then prayer can be something of a smoke screen. The call to prayer may be for the membership to be more generous but also that the leaders will lead in this vital aspect of ministry. Jeremiah warned that the spiritual leaders of his day 'dress the wound of my people as though it were not serious' (Jeremiah 8:11).

Every clergyman will tell you the same story: the rich are usually the very worst when it comes to giving. 'Poor' people give far more than the rich. Every minister knows that commitment produces more money than just wealth alone, but few ministers will act upon Paul's word to Timothy:

> Command those who are rich in this present world ... to do good, to be rich in good deeds, and to be generous and willing to share. **1 Timothy 6: 17 - 19**

In 1993 there was a new initiative in Britain by the Church of England to raise the level of giving by its members. The church had been lulled into a false sense of security as for many years it had relied upon the Church Commissioners to make a major contribution to clergy stipends. The church had been living off the proceeds of the past - the sacrifice and commitment of previous generations and the land acquired over centuries. A crisis had arisen and there was the possibility of having to cut back on the number of clergy or reducing the number of parishes or both. In what was the Decade of Evangelism there was talk of retreat when expansion was the aim.

The problem was not money.

The members of the church are rich; they drive good cars, go on overseas holidays, live in centrally heated homes with dishwashers, TVs, DVDs and computers, and some even send their children to schools costing tens of thousands of pounds a year. In April 2007 'Churchgoing in the UK' a research survey conducted for Tearfund revealed that churchgoing is associated with those of higher social grade. Adults in social grades AB have above average prevalence of regular churchgoers (22% and 21% respectively). Adults in grades C2 and D have the lowest proportion at 12%. The situation is reminiscent of that after the return from Exile when the Israelites had started rebuilding the Temple and God spoke through the prophet Haggai:

This is what the Lord Almighty says: 'These people say, "The time has not yet come for the Lord's house to be built."'

Then the word of the Lord came through the prophet Haggai: 'Is it a time for you yourselves to be living in your panelled houses, while this house remains a ruin?'

Now this is what the Lord Almighty says: 'Give careful thought to your ways. You have planted much, but have harvested little. You eat, but never have enough. You drink, but never have your fill. You put on clothes, but are not warm. You earn wages, only to put them in a purse with holes in it.'

This is what the Lord Almighty says: 'Give careful thought to your ways. Go up into the mountains and bring down timber and build the house, so that I may take pleasure in it and be honoured,' says the Lord.

'You expected much, but see, it turned out to be little. What you brought home, I blew away. Why?' declares the Lord Almighty. 'Because of my house, which remains a ruin, while each of you is busy with his own house.' **Haggai 1: 2 - 9**

The picture is clear. The Israelites are back in Jerusalem where, under the benevolent dictatorship of King Darius, they have been permitted to rebuild the Temple. But for all their longing while sitting beside the rivers of Babylon, they have not restored the Temple, their work is incomplete, half-finished. Why? Because they have set themselves up in panelled houses!

What is the significance of 'panelled houses'? In Old Testament times poor people smeared mud on the walls of their houses; those with some money used lime to whitewash the walls; but the wealthy put up wooden panelling.

The panelled houses of the Old Testament are surely the centrally heated, two-car homes of today equipped with dishwashers, TVs, DVDs and computers. The members of the Church in most western countries are wealthy, while the Church is 'in ruins'.

One might assume, therefore, that this book is a manual on how to increase the giving in a church by a new type of fundraising campaign. It is not. It is not a book on methodology but of principles. It is not even a book about fundraising - *often erroneously called 'stewardship'*. It is a book about stewards and a basic premise of the book is that every Christian is a steward.

Principles must come before methodology. The latter will vary according to a number of factors, for each church has different needs, responsibilities and opportunities.

Writing a book about the ideal planned giving campaign is impossible, writing a book about the possible variations in a campaign would be difficult and lengthy. A book on principles is simpler and can be used as a study guide for personal or group work or for a campaign. The early chapters of the book in particular reflect the 'study guide' style to make them easy to use for home groups.

However, my primary purpose in writing this book is to stimulate individual Christians to a careful and prayerful reconsideration of their own role as stewards. Writing it has been an extremely soul-searching exercise and I have considered the implications in my own life. A number of things have had to change.

Two other points need to be made. Firstly, my main concern is that our position as stewards needs re-emphasis. This, I propose, falls into three categories: earth, ethics and evangelism. I am not an expert in these areas and so the reader may well feel that further reading is necessary.

The trinity of earth, ethics and evangelism is like that of faith, hope and love. You cannot consider one part to the exclusion of the others. So, while it is convenient to treat each one separately, they should also be considered together. If, for example, as stewards of the earth we utilise the soil in the right way we will have enough food to feed everyone. As stewards of ethics we will want to ensure that it is properly distributed and no one is exploited - whether it be the labourer, the farmer, or those who cannot afford to pay the current market price. As stewards of evangelism we will seek to proclaim that man does not live by bread alone unless it be the Bread of the New Covenant, the Lord Jesus Christ.

Secondly, this book grew in the writing. It seemed that it was raising its own questions and they had to be answered. As a result there are a few chapters that were added along the way - such as those on legacies and the theology of giving. Neither is meant to be comprehensive, though both are of particular interest to me. The National Lottery in the UK also raises questions and so finds its way into the book. In a sense these later chapters cover the practical implications of what it means to be a steward in a world constantly facing new challenges and questions.

CHAPTER 1
The cart before the horse

Stewardship is not primarily about money. Stewardship is not even about time, talents and treasure. Stewardship is a relationship, a very special relationship with a very special person.

This is a book about stewards and then about stewardship. In the Bible there are many references to stewards but only three to stewardship. The biblical emphasis is first and foremost on what we are and then on what we do. Stewardship is the end product, put into practice by stewards. When we concentrate on stewardship we lose a lot of the force of the biblical teaching about stewards - use of the abstract noun can become just that - abstract.

Stewards are God's people. So to begin we must focus on people - on those who make up the relationship - the Lord Jesus Christ and the stewards.

Before we go any further, we must have it clear in our minds as to who are stewards in the Church. We are not referring to those people who take up the offering or show you to your seat. They are not stewards in the biblical sense, as we shall see. Who then are stewards? Are they a specific group in the Church?

There is considerable confusion in the Church about certain names or descriptions given to Christians in the New Testament. Do they all apply to me? Where do I fit in? Some of those names are: believers, converts, apostles, witnesses, speakers in tongues, evangelists, prophets, healers, pastors, priests, soldiers, disciples, saints, slaves, teachers and stewards.

The list is not complete but it is really a mixture of two groups: firstly those words which describe each and every Christian and then those words that describe a gift of the Spirit or an appointment in the Church (there is some overlap between these two groups), words that apply to some Christians but not to others. The two groups are:

Group 1	Group 2
converts	apostles
believers	speakers in tongues
disciples	evangelists
witnesses	prophets
priests	people with a gift of healing
saints	pastor/teachers
slaves	
soldiers	
stewards	

The second group is a list of some of the gifts of the Spirit apportioned as He wills (1 Corinthians 12:11), 'to prepare God's people for works of service, so that the body of Christ may be built up until we all reach unity in the faith and the knowledge of the son of God and become mature, attaining to the whole measure of the fullness of Christ' (Ephesians 4: 12, 13).

There is an interesting verse at the beginning of Paul's discourse on the gifts of the Spirit in 1 Corinthians 12:

> There are different kinds of gifts, but the same Spirit. There are different kinds of service, but the same Lord. There are different kinds of working, but the same God works all of them in all men. **1 Corinthians 12: 4-6**

There is a trinity here:

> gifts and Spirit;
> service and Lord;
> working and God.

The odd one out is the third one, which specifically states that while there are different kinds of working they are common to all Christians for *'God works all of them in all men'*. Later in his letter Paul implies that Christians have different gifts and indeed different areas of service but 'workings' are common to us all.

These verses are an important clue in the interpretation of the chapters on the gifts of the Spirit. In 1 Corinthians 12 the first list is of gifts (vv 8-10), while the second is of appointments to the body of Christ and indicates areas of ministry or service (v 28). In verses 29 to 31 Paul draws both groups together and encourages us to 'eagerly desire the greater gifts'. In his thinking all gifts come from God; even the privilege of service is a gift from God. Clearly a gift implies service for with the gift comes the responsibility to use it in his service. But underpinning both gifts and service is the fact that God is working in every Christian in every way. The three are not separate issues but intimately linked.

The Church is made up of a vast army of men and women who are all working for God our Father, each with his or her own gifts and areas of service. The link that holds them together is love and Paul makes this very clear in 1 Corinthians 13. We maintain the unity of the Spirit through the fruit of the Spirit. The Church is effective when we work together, using our gifts in his service and evidencing the fruit of the Spirit in our lives.

But whereas gifts and areas of service differ for each and every Christian, <u>our concern is with something that affects all Christians</u>. There are many names given to Christians which are common to us all - and one of them is 'stewards'. For this is not a book for a special or select group of Christians but is intended for all who believe in the Lord Jesus Christ.

It is important to understand that all Christians share the same basic relationships with the Lord. So we must take a brief look at the different aspects of this relationship as they also have bearing on some of the areas of stewardship we will be looking at in later chapters. From Scripture it is clear that every Christian is a

- convert,
- believer,

- saint,
- disciple,
- priest,
- slave,
- witness,
- soldier,
- steward.

These words all reflect some aspect of the dynamic relationship between every Christian and the Lord Jesus Christ.

Convert

Every Christian is a *convert* from a way of life that was self-centred to one acknowledging Jesus as Lord. 'You were taught, with regard to your former way of life to put off your old self, which is being corrupted by its deceitful desires; to be made new in the attitude of your minds; and to put on the new self, created to be like God in true righteousness and holiness'. (Ephesians 4: 22 - 24). This is also an on-going process as we are not to be conformed to this world but are to be continually transformed by the renewal of our minds (Romans 12: 2). Conversion is both an initial experience and a continual process as we surrender ourselves to his lordship.

Believer

Every Christian is a *believer*, one who has put his or her faith in the Lord Jesus Christ. By definition we are all converts and believers - otherwise we are not Christians. Belief and trust are things that grow. The Apostles' Creed sums up the beliefs of the Church and for some reading it is, at first, merely part of the ritual of Sunday worship, then reading becomes recitation and finally (hopefully) it turns into the realisation that '*I* believe in God the Father Almighty, maker of heaven and earth, and in Jesus Christ his only Son, *my* Lord.' Our faith may be weak and we may echo the apostles when they said to the Lord: 'Increase our faith!' His reply remains the same: 'If you have faith as small as a mustard seed, you can say to this mulberry tree, "Be uprooted and planted in the sea," and it will obey you.' The Christian's cry will always be: 'I do believe; help me overcome my unbelief' (Mark 9: 24).

Saint

Every Christian is a *saint*. This emerges particularly clearly from the letters of the Apostle Paul where he regularly addresses all Christians as saints. Being a saint is part of the concept of holiness, being set apart or separated from the profane for divine service. This is why being a saint and being a slave are not mutually exclusive concepts. Both have to do with service, a relationship between the servant and his or her master. As slaves we have been purchased, 'you were bought at a price' (1 Corinthians 6: 20) and are now owned by a new Master, and as saints we have been appointed to His Majesty's Service. As slaves and saints we are, at the same time, both the lowest estate and privileged to serve the King of Kings. The fact that we are saints does not mean we are perfect but that we are in service - and each and every Christian has been set apart for God's service - 'Better is one day in your courts than a thousand elsewhere; I would rather be a doorkeeper in the house of my God than dwell in the tents of the wicked' (Psalm 84:10).

Disciple

Every Christian is a *disciple*, one who has met with the Lord Jesus Christ and, having met him, has committed his life to following the example of his Master. Disciples seek to emulate their leader, to discipline their lives by him and his teaching. Christianity is not so much a set of rules to be observed but a life lived in harmony with the Lord Jesus Christ. His disciples have always been students of the Scriptures for it is in the written Word that we find Jesus, the Living Word. Disciples frequently fail but because they are in a loving relationship with their Lord they know he forgives them and they 'press on toward the goal to win the prize for which God has called [us] heavenward in Christ Jesus' (Philippians 3: 14).

Priest

Every Christian is a *priest*. The doctrine known as 'the priesthood of all believers' is based on Peter's words in his first epistle, 'But you are a chosen people, a royal priesthood, a holy nation, a people belonging to God, that you may declare the praises of him who called you out of darkness into his wonderful light' (1 Peter 2: 9). Peter was quoting from the Old Testament, God's words to Moses on Mount Sinai, 'Although the whole earth is mine, you will be for me a kingdom of priests and a holy nation' (Exodus 19: 5 & 6). God honoured the Israelites by making them a special people and according to the Apostle Peter; Christians have taken on that role. Priests approach God on behalf of the people, offering praise, prayer and sacrifice. The sacrifice we offer is '[y]our bodies as living sacrifices, holy and pleasing to God - which is [y]our spiritual worship' (Romans 12: 1). We should be priests in our worship of God, praising him and offering prayer for the nations and on their behalf. Intercessory prayer has always been an important part of the life of the Church and needs to be re-emphasised in a world that continues to face turmoil, unrest and violence. The Apostle Paul also refers to his 'priestly duty of proclaiming the gospel of God, so that the Gentiles might become an offering acceptable to God, sanctified by the Holy Spirit' (Romans 15: 16).

Slave

Slaves were common right across the Roman Empire. Slavery had been in existence for thousands of years and in diverse cultures. Common to the situation all slaves were owned by their masters and had very few rights. The master expected total obedience. Because the master/slave relationship was so familiar to everyone Paul used it to explain the state of sinners and their relationship to the Lord Jesus Christ. Paul wrote, 'Don't you know that when you offer yourselves to someone to obey him as slaves, you are slaves to the one whom you obey-whether you are slaves to sin, which leads to death, or to obedience, which leads to righteousness? But thanks be to God that, though you used to be slaves to sin, you wholeheartedly obeyed the form of teaching to which you were entrusted. You have been set free from sin and have become slaves to righteousness ... you have been set free from sin and have become slaves to God' (Romans 6: 16-18, 22). As slaves we acknowledge the lordship of our Saviour. We confirm it when we sing, 'All to Jesus I surrender, all to Him I freely give'.

There is a lovely picture in the Old Testament of the slave who loves his master. Israelites could have a fellow Israelite as a slave but after six years the slave had to be set free. 'And when you release him, do not send him away empty-handed. Supply him liberally from your flock, your threshing floor and your winepress. Give to him as the Lord your God has blessed you. But if your servant says to you, "I do not want to leave you," because he loves you and your family and is well off with you, then take an awl and push it through his ear lobe into the door, and he will become your servant for life' (Deuteronomy 15: 13, 14 & 16). This is a picture of the new relationship between the Lord Jesus Christ and the slaves he calls 'friends'.

Witness

Every Christian is a *witness*. Our witness is to the Lord Jesus Christ and the purpose of our witness is to draw people to him. Our lives should be so attractive that people ask us to give account of the hope that is in us (1 Peter 3: 15). Nevertheless, this is an area that troubles many Christians. 'I can't witness' is an often-heard cry, but what is generally meant is 'I can't evangelise.' Christians are witnesses whether they realise it or not. Our lives, our conversation, all act as a witness, either drawing people to Jesus or turning them away. Jesus said: 'He who is not with me is against me, and *he who does not gather with me, scatters*' (Luke 11: 23). Going to church is an act of witness, especially in countries where the Church is persecuted. The fact is I am either a good witness or a bad witness, for there is no such thing as a non-witnessing Christian. A negative attitude to witnessing will inevitably result in a bad witness.

Soldier

Every Christian is a *soldier*. We are all commanded to put on the full armour of God in our fight against the devil (Ephesians 6:11, 13). The Lord Jesus prophesied that the gates of hell would not withstand the attack of the Church he was to build (Matthew 16:18). No Christian has doubted that he or she is involved in spiritual warfare - we have fought against the world, the flesh and the devil. Our hymns bear testimony to it: 'Onward, Christian soldiers, marching as to war', 'Soldiers of Christ arise...' William Booth's motivation in founding the Salvation Army was his desire to mobilise soldiers for Christ's cause. However, with the rise of militant Islam we must emphasise the fact that nowhere in the New Testament did Jesus even suggest that force is a way to extend his kingdom. When Christians are persecuted we are commanded not to retaliate. Rather we are to 'Love [y]our enemies and pray for those who persecute you, that you may be sons of your Father in heaven (Matthew 5: 44, 45).

Steward

Every Christian is a *steward*. Jesus often used stories about stewards as illustrations in his teaching ministry. He never suggested that stewards form an elite group different from other Christians. There is never any suggestion that only some of his followers would be stewards and others not. The steward is an extension of the slave/servant concept. We will be looking at the story of the three stewards in Matthew 25 in the next chapter. They had different talents but they were all stewards. The New Testament does not teach us that stewards were the upper hierarchy of the Church. Stewardship is a relationship between every Christian and the Lord - not a specific role in the Church.

The details of that relationship are the subject of this book. It may not be clear to you that you are a steward. Please proceed with an open mind as we look into Scripture to discover what the Word has to say about this important truth; every Christian is a steward. Every Christian needs to wake up to the fact that

**we are either good stewards or bad stewards –
for there is no such thing as a Christian who is not a steward.**

You cannot ignore or deny that which is an integral part of your relationship with your Lord. If we are honest most of us will admit that we are ignorant of the implications of our responsibilities as stewards and therefore are probably bad stewards.

The distinction between being stewards and stewardship is not an academic one but is vital to the well being of the Church. Churches have run 'stewardship campaigns' for years in an effort to boost income and most have been successful to some degree. Often they have only approached the active members of the congregation and the impression is given that stewardship is for certain members only. It becomes an optional extra, something we can agree to do or ignore if we so wish. It is for the 'committed' membership. As a result we never come to grips with the truth that all Christians are stewards.

There is a need to educate all Christians so that they recognise that they are stewards, grasp the implications of this in all areas of life and make a commitment to be better stewards.

The Church must get its own house in order. Apathetic members do a lot of harm to the Church as they perpetuate the notion that you can be a Christian without commitment. These people are often the hardest to reach but we owe it to them and to the Lord to make the effort - their testimony is a damaging witness and hard to refute; 'I go to church from time to time and it does nothing for me.' *Apathy is a greater problem for the Church than atheism.*

Every Christian is a convert, a believer, a saint, a disciple, a priest, a slave, a witness, a soldier and also a steward. Most accept the first eight in one way or another but because we have taught steward*ship* we have forgotten or just do not realise that we are all stewards. Christians, who have neglected this aspect of their relationship with the Lord, have the potential to revitalise the Church, bringing renewal both locally and around the world.

QUESTIONS

- Are you a Christian? Are you sure? How would you prove it from the Bible?

- How far have you come as a Christian? Consider the nine characteristics one-by-one, where are you in your pilgrimage?

    Convert, believer and saint are indications of your state as a Christian.

    Disciple, priest and slave are indications of service – usually within the Church.

    Witness, soldier and steward are indications of your ministry in the world.

CHAPTER 2
What is a steward?

If all Christians are stewards we must now consider the question, 'What is a steward?'

Please do not be tempted to skip this section because the format seems familiar. It must form the basis of our understanding about stewards and is a vital part of our study.

Confusion can arise as the word 'steward' has a number of different meanings. The common ones are:

1. The paid manager of an estate or great house, a person entrusted with the management of someone else's property

2. The person responsible for provisions in a college, club, or ship

3. An official managing a race meeting, ball, or show

4. A passengers' attendant or waiter on a ship or aircraft

5. A trade union representative or shop steward.

Churches often have people to show visitors to their seats and to take up the offering at worship services. They are often called 'stewards' or 'door-stewards'. In the church I grew up in it was quite common to hear the minister say, 'Would the stewards please come forward to take up the offering.' But the fact is that the stewards are the ones in the pews, not those taking up the offering!

The purpose of this book is to rediscover the importance that the Bible places on the role of stewards in the life of the Church. And so as to avoid confusion we should call door-stewards by another name, either 'helpers' or 'ushers'.

The second and third meanings in the above list are specific applications of the principle found in the first meaning, which is derived from Old English and is also the biblical meaning found in the teaching of the Lord Jesus. Steward comes from *stig* 'a house' and *weard* 'a warden', hence **'person entrusted with the management of another's property'**.

The 'Parable of the Talents'

It is appropriate, therefore, to consider the parable found in Matthew 25: 14-30. This story is usually called 'the parable of the talents' and this is the heading given by the editors of the New International Version. But it has very little to do with talents. It is really 'the story of the stewards'.

'Again, it will be like a man going on a journey, who called his servants and entrusted his property to them. To one he gave five talents of money, to another two talents, and to another one talent, each according to his ability. Then he went on his journey. The man who had received the five talents went at once and put his money to work and gained five more. So also, the one with two talents gained two more. But the man who had received the one talent went off, dug a hole in the ground and hid his master's money.

After a long time the master of those servants returned and settled accounts with them. The man who had received the five talents brought the other five. "Master," he said, "you entrusted me with five talents. See, I have gained five more."

His master replied, "Well done, good and faithful servant! You have been faithful with a few things; I will put you in charge of many things. Come and share your master's happiness."

The man with the two talents also came. "Master," he said, "you entrusted me with two talents; see, I have gained two more."

His master replied, "Well done, good and faithful servant! You have been faithful with a few things; I will put you in charge of many things. Come and share your master's happiness!"

Then the man who had received the one talent came.

"Master," he said, "I knew that you were a hard man, harvesting where you have not sown and gathering where you have not scattered seed. So I was afraid and went out and hid your talent in the ground. See, here is what belongs to you."

His master replied, "You wicked, lazy servant! So you knew that I harvest where I have not sown and gather where I have not scattered seed? Well then, you should have put my money on deposit with the bankers, so that when I returned I would have received it back with interest. Take the talent from him and give it to the one who has the ten talents. For everyone who has will be given more, and he will have an abundance. Whoever does not have, even what he has will be taken from him. And throw that worthless servant outside, into the darkness, where there will be weeping and gnashing of teeth."

All the elements of the relationship between master and steward are contained in this story and so it deserves our close attention. There are a number of principles in this parable but they all relate to one theme: what it is to be a steward.

The basic elements are the owner and his servants and their relationship and this can be portrayed as follows:

Owner (God) delegates authority in his absence to the

Servant (me) who is appointed to be a steward as he accepts responsibility for managing the property in the owner's absence and gives account to the

Owner (God) when he returns and rewards his

Steward (me) according to his management of the property.

The four essential elements are:

God	AUTHORITY
Steward	RESPONSIBILITY
Steward	ACCOUNTABILITY
God	REWARD

Those in business will recognise that this is a basic management principle. Or to draw a modern comparison: the owner or shareholders of a company appoint a person to manage the company and at the end of each year to give account of the company's profitability. Depending on whether the company makes a loss or a profit, the manager can expect to be censured or even fired, or receive a bonus.

The principles that are to be found in this parable will be applied throughout the book and so we will deal with them one by one.

PRINCIPLE 1 - Relationship

The basic principle is that there is *a relationship between two people*. The people are not equals; the one is the owner and the other his servant. Throughout the relationship the owner maintains his ownership of his property, he does not give it to the servant. However, in the owner's absence the servant is appointed to the position of a steward. On the owner's return the faithful steward enters into a new relationship with the owner.

PRINCIPLE 2 - Authority

In his absence the owner delegates *authority* to the servant, thus enabling him to act as a steward. The steward acts on the owner's behalf and in the owner's best interests. There is a clear distinction between a servant and a steward as a servant has no authority - he merely carries out his master's orders. Stewards do not behave like servants but as representatives of the owner and do so with his authority.

PRINCIPLE 3 - Responsibility

Implicit in the change from servant to steward is the acceptance of *responsibility*. The steward recognises that he is responsible for the owner's property in the owner's absence. His loyalty is to the owner and he does all that is within his power to ensure that the property earns the maximum return during the time the owner is away. There is no passing the buck to someone else. At a time when the concept of personal responsibility for one's actions is not popular, this is a very important consideration as we look at the steward's role in the Church.

PRINCIPLE 4 - Accountability

Intertwined with responsibility is *accountability*. The steward accepts that one day he will have to give an account of his stewardship. There is a day of reckoning. The third servant in the parable accepted the responsibility when he received the one talent but fear kept him from doing anything, even though he knew he was accountable for the talent. Accountability to God is not a popular concept in many circles. There is a superficial Christianity that proclaims that we are saved by grace and have an insurance policy guaranteeing entrance to heaven and the promise of eternal, abundant life regardless of what we do or don't do in this life. Provided we try to abstain from sin we are all right. Being stewards means we will have to give account of what we have done with God's gifts in positive action to achieve the owner's goals - not burying our talents in the ground.

PRINCIPLE 5 - Reward

Stewards are *rewarded* for their achievements - or lack of them. Again this is not a popular idea - that there is reward or discipline according to the service rendered. In business this is accepted and even expected - that we should be rewarded for good service and if we fail to do our job then we can expect to be disciplined or even dismissed. Undoubtedly God is fair, righteous and loving in dealing with his children, but no child should presume on the Father's love. Our works cannot save us, but having been saved by faith in the Son of God, let us work out our salvation with fear and trembling for it is God who works in us to will and to act according to his good purpose (Philippians 2: 12, 13). More on accountability and rewards will be found in Chapters 13 and 14.

PRINCIPLE 6 - All servants are stewards

According to the parable *all the servants are appointed stewards*.

There are three servants with different talents or status but they are all made stewards. This is in keeping with our earlier statement that all Christians are stewards. If, therefore, you have read through the first five principles and decided that they are not for you, then perhaps you will have to go back and ensure that you understand and accept that these principles do apply to you. There is a sense in which all Christians are servants, even slaves, but that is a separate aspect of our relationship with our Father. Slaves obey orders - that is the primary requirement. But as Christians we are expected to use our initiative in his service. So if all Christians have to give account of their works it is because they are all stewards.

PRINCIPLE 7 - Differing abilities

Stewards have *different abilities*. We are all different and our Father treats us as individuals, according to the gifts and talents he has given us. Some of these gifts are hereditary, others come from the circumstances of our upbringing, and still others are directly from him. We are all capable of contributing to the Kingdom of God in one way or another. And yet the argument persists, often from intelligent, successful people, that they cannot help as they have nothing to offer. They are, in effect, calling God a liar as he has given them certain abilities and expects them to use those gifts in his service. Every Christian has God-given abilities and with his help those gifts can be developed, 'And God is able to make all grace abound to you, so that in all things at all times, having all that you need, you will abound in every good work' (2 Corinthians 9: 8). Please note that the more God gives us the greater is our responsibility.

PRINCIPLE 8 - Reciprocal giving

Christian giving is *reciprocal giving*. The owner makes his contribution first and then the steward builds on it. We give in response to God's love: 'Not that we loved God, but that he [first] loved us and sent his Son as an atoning sacrifice for our sins' (1 John 4: 10). God took the initiative and 'while we were still sinners,

Christ died for us' (Romans 5: 8). The Cross is the proof of God's love and he paid the price that we were not able to pay. There is nothing that we can do to repay him; we are indebted to God's grace for new life, abundant life and eternal life. W C Grace declared:

> If Christ be God and he died for me,
> then nothing he asks can be too much
> for me to do for him.

Charities appeal for support on the basis of their need. The Church should not. Christians do not, or should not, give firstly because there is a need, no matter how lofty the cause. Christians give primarily out of gratitude for God's love and in obedience to Christ's command.

One of the most demeaning activities of the Church is the way in which its leaders, in an effort to increase income, are reduced to begging from the members (even worse from non-members) to meet a shortfall or a pile of debts. Fetes, coffee mornings, cake sales, bingo drives, etc. etc. are a further trivialisation of the Gospel and unworthy of the Church and its Lord.

If a congregation's giving far exceeds the local need, then the 'excess' can be used for the missionary work of the Church. The principle of 'wealthier' congregations helping their less affluent brothers and sisters occurs early in the life of the Church. The Christians in Antioch, Corinth and Macedonia all contributed to the needs of the Church in Jerusalem (Acts 11: 28-30, 2 Corinthians 9: 1-5). 'Now, however, I am on my way to Jerusalem in the service of the saints there. For Macedonia and Achaia were pleased to make a contribution for the poor among the saints in Jerusalem' (Romans 15: 25, 26).

PRINCIPLE 9 - Value of individual contributions

What return on investment was acceptable to the owner in the parable? The principle here is both interesting and crucial to matters we shall consider later.

Both the first and the second stewards gave a return of 100 per cent. Their contribution equalled that of their master. He gave all he had (all his property was distributed to his servants) and they responded by matching his contribution. This is an exciting concept - for Jesus is saying that *our individual contributions are valuable and important* - as valuable as his contribution. Those who feel that their gifts are insignificant and cannot make a difference should reconsider, for the Lord needs each one of us, as we are all part of his plan for the Church.

Notice also that both the first and second steward achieved the same return. It did not matter that the first one had gained five talents and the second only two, both had a 100 per cent return. It is the same in business. It is the profit margin that is important, as £1,000,000 in profits may be 20 per cent of turnover for one company but only 2 per cent for another. In business profitability is measured as a percentage of turnover. With its emphasis on percentage giving (the tithe), the Old Testament is remarkably up to date.

Those Christians who feel that their contribution is small and that others, more gifted than themselves, will get all the praise in heaven should take heart. God looks at our motives and commitment, not the size of our gift. The stewards received the same commendation because they had achieved the same target and this principle applies to all Christians.

PRINCIPLE 10 - Generosity

The tithe is often used as a basis for Christian giving, even though the New Testament does not use the tithe in this way. Nowhere in the New Testament are Christians told to tithe - *generosity* is the foundation of Christian giving. Isaac Watts, the hymn writer, sums up this principle:

> Were the whole realm of nature mine,
> that were an offering far too small,
> Love so amazing, so divine,
> Demands my life, my soul, my all.

In the parable the first two stewards made every effort to ensure that they fulfilled their responsibility. Their aim was to please their master and to satisfy his demands. They gave their all to achieve their goal and as pointed out in Principle 9 their return was 100 per cent. If we are to talk of percentage giving we should realise that the level that the master found acceptable was 100 per cent.

In sending out his disciples, Jesus commanded them, 'Freely you have received, freely give' (Matthew 10: 8). This is the hallmark of the Christian who understands that all that he has is a gift from God and therefore nothing is his own - he is a steward entrusted by God to use his gifts in the Lord's service. His attitude is not miserly but generous. If 'God loves a cheerful giver' then it is difficult to see how we can give a miserly amount in a cheerful manner - unless we are misers!

In the Gospels two people stand out for being commended by Jesus, one he knew well and the other perhaps not at all. Of the first he said, 'There has not risen anyone greater than John the Baptist' (Matthew 11: 11), and of the second, 'I tell you the truth, this poor widow has put more into the treasury than all the others. They all gave out of their wealth; but she, out of her poverty, put in everything - all she had to live on' (Mark 12: 43, 44). Both gave all that they had in their service and devotion to God.

These ten principles are fundamental to being a steward, fundamental to being a Christian. They have been listed in the order that they appear in the parable but can be summarised as follows:

1. All Christians are stewards.
2. Stewards are in a special relationship with their Master, and that relationship is governed by four main principles:
3. Authority
4. Responsibility
5. Accountability
6. Reward

Moreover stewards have

7.   Different abilities but
8.   All our contributions are valuable and important, and are based on
9.   Reciprocal giving, which is characterised by
10.   Generosity.

We must now look at the application of these principles in the lives of people in the Bible. They will provide the basis for our understanding of what it means to be a steward in the service of the Lord Jesus Christ.

QUESTIONS

- What was your definition of a steward before reading this chapter?

- How has it changed?

- How would you rate yourself for taking responsibility for your words, your actions and your beliefs?

- What responsibilities do you have as a Christian?

- What responsibilities does your church have?

CHAPTER 3
The perfect steward

The Christian's example is the Lord Jesus Christ. The Apostle Paul's cry was, 'I want to know Christ and the power of his resurrection and the fellowship of sharing in his sufferings, becoming like him in his death' (Philippians 3: 10). Becoming like Christ involves not merely the example of his life but also that of the loving sacrifice of his death. Peter wrote, 'To this end you were called, because Christ suffered for you, leaving you an example, that you should follow in his steps' (1 Peter 2: 21).

If we are to follow the Lord Jesus Christ as our example in all of life, what evidence is there in Scripture of Christ as the perfect steward? The evidence of the Gospels portrays Jesus as a steward in his relationship with his Father. All four aspects are present: authority, responsibility, accountability and reward.

God the Father has the authority. Jesus acknowledged that authority throughout his earthly ministry, 'I do nothing on my own but speak just what the Father has taught me. The one who sent me is with me; he has not left me alone, for I always do what pleases him' (John 8: 28 & 29).

Confirmation of Jesus' appointment as a steward occurred in very special circumstances. After his baptism, while Jesus was praying 'heaven was opened, and the Holy Spirit descended on him in bodily form, as a dove, and a voice came from heaven, "You are my beloved Son; with whom I am well pleased"' (Luke 3: 21, 22). And later on the Mount of Transfiguration this was confirmed with the addition of a new dimension, 'This is my beloved Son, with whom I am well pleased; listen to him' (Matthew 17: 5).

God the Father recognised Jesus as his Son at his baptism and for the disciples this was a clear testimony of the unique relationship between Father and Son. The Son represented the Father, and had his approval, which showed that he was acting with his Father's authority. This was confirmed at the Mount of Transfiguration in the Father's command: 'Listen to him.' Jesus spoke with the Father's authority: 'For I have come down from heaven not to do my will but to do the will of him who sent me' (John 6: 38).

He did this in all three areas we will consider in later chapters. He did this by reaffirming God's sovereignty

- over the earth - in Matthew 6: 26 - 30 Jesus uses both fauna and flora as illustrations and shows his concern for created things

- in ethics - 'Do not think that I have come to abolish the Law or the Prophets; I have not come to abolish them but to fulfil them' (Matthew 5: 17)

- and to establish God's kingdom through the Gospel, indeed he is the Gospel, the Evangel.

Right up to the end Jesus was accountable to his Father, 'Abba, Father, everything is possible for you. Take this cup from me. Yet not what I will, but what you will' (Mark 14: 36). When, on the Cross, he cried, 'It is finished!' he did so because he had completed the task he had been sent to do. He had been given the responsibility for the salvation of the world. He did it. Though it cost him his life, he did not flinch from his task but 'became obedient to death - even death on a cross!' (Philippians 2: 8). And he gave account before His Father, 'For Christ did not enter a man-made sanctuary that was only a copy of the true one; he entered heaven itself, now to appear for us in God's presence' (Hebrews 11: 24).

Jesus received the reward of the perfect steward, 'Therefore God exalted him to the highest place and gave him the name that is above every name, that at the name of Jesus every knee should bow, in heaven and on earth and under the earth, and every tongue confess that Jesus Christ is Lord, to the glory of God the Father' (Philippians 2: 9 - 11).

An interesting distinction is apparent in the way in which the

Gospels portray Jesus as a steward sent from God. In the Synoptic Gospels Jesus communicates in the main through parables. Some parables are about stewards and our Lord has a part to play in these parables, often as the agent of his Father. It does not take careful reading to see that Jesus acknowledged that he was a steward as well.

But in John's Gospel he makes a direct claim - that of being his Father's steward. The change in emphasis is quite clear. In Matthew, Mark and Luke we have parables about stewards. In John's Gospel, Jesus makes very clear claims to be his Father's steward in a number of instances while in others his language is characterised by stewardship terminology. The following list of references from John's Gospel gives an idea of the wide support that there is for claiming that Jesus saw himself as a steward in relationship with his Father. Take the verses in chapter 3 as an example.

Verse 17:   For God did not send His son into the world to condemn the world, but to save the world through him.

Verse 32:   He testifies to what he has seen and heard, but no one accepts his testimony.

Verse 34:   For the one whom God has sent speaks the words of God; to him God gives the Spirit without limit.

Verse 35:   The Father loves the Son and has placed everything in his hands.

The following verses illustrate that the Lord Jesus was sent with his Father's authority and he took responsibility for the task he was given.

Chapter   3: 17, 32, 34, 35
          4: 34
          5: 17, 19, 22, 27, 30, 36, 43
          6: 38
          8: 29
          9: 4

Chapter   10: 18
           12: 44 - 50
           13: 3
           14: 10, 31
           15: 1 – 17 (the vine and branches)
           16: 12 - 15 (the Holy Spirit as steward)
           17: 2, 4, 7, 8, 18
           18: 11
           20: 19 - 22.

The teaching on the vine and the branches in John 15 is an interesting parallel with the parables in the Synoptic Gospels. Jesus often used the vineyard as the setting for his parables about stewards in Matthew, Mark and Luke. But in John 15 he gives us an insight into the meaning behind the parables and takes the disciples a step further: if we remain in him as he is in the Father, we will bear much fruit and bring glory to the Father just as Jesus always sought his Father's glory. Jesus goes on to tell the disciples the most amazing thing in verse 15: 'I no longer call you servants, because a servant does not know his master's business. Instead, I have called you friends, for everything that I learned from my Father I have made known to you.' Jesus is telling his disciples that they have been given a major change in status; they have moved from being servants (slaves in the Greek) to being his friends. Like the steward the friends of the steward are to 'go and bear fruit - fruit that will last'. This is the same kind of fruit that Jesus came to produce.

In the second half of the chapter, from verse 18 onwards, Jesus warns his disciples that, as his stewards, they will be persecuted just as he was persecuted. This also fits the pattern of the parable of the vineyard where the owner finally sends his son and the tenants kill the son.

From verse 26 and on into Chapter 16, Jesus explains the role of the Holy Spirit within the context of what he has said in Chapter 15. The wording from verse 12 to verse 15 of Chapter 16 is almost identical to that used by Jesus to explain his relationship with the

Father as a steward - so there can be no doubt that he intends us to understand that the Holy Spirit is in a similar relationship as a steward and is to be the power and counsel for the disciples so that they can fulfil their calling as stewards!

When he appeared to the disciples after his resurrection, Jesus said, 'As the Father has sent me, I am sending you. And with that he breathed on them and said, Receive the Holy Spirit' (John 20: 21, 22). This is virtually a summary of what he has said in Chapters 15 and 16.

One further observation must be made about the parables in the Synoptic Gospels. The writers record Jesus as using the opportunity to answer the question, 'What will be the sign of your coming and of the end of the age?' to tell a number of parables about stewards and to highlight the accountability aspect of stewardship. As he knew that he would soon have to give account to his Father so he warned the disciples that they would also have to give account to the Father. The parables about stewards occur at the end of the Gospels, after Jesus has gone to Jerusalem for the last time, knowing that the end was near. There is a balance between the exciting prospect of the Lord's return and our responsibility to be his stewards until we hear the trumpet call. Christianity was never escapism to never-never land; it was always crucifixion before resurrection, a crown of thorns before the crown of the King.

QUESTIONS

* What is the difference between the Lord Jesus as a steward and a Christian as a steward?

* Have you looked up the verses in John's Gospel?

* Using these verses write up your own thoughts on the Lord Jesus as the perfect steward.

CHAPTER 4
Three stewards

Three people in the Bible exemplify the extent of our Christian responsibility as stewards: Adam, Moses and Jesus - Adam in terms of the earth, Moses for ethics and the Lord Jesus for evangelism.

We begin by looking at the basic principles in this chapter but examine the implications in a little more detail in the next three chapters.

Adam

Adam was the first steward in the Bible. In the beginning God created the heavens and the earth. He 'breathed into [man's] nostrils the breath of life, and man became a living being' (Gen 2: 7). The apex of God's creation was someone 'in his own image'. Because man was created in the image of God, God could put him in control of his creation. Clearly He had the authority to do so and Adam accepted the responsibility under the very clear conditions laid down by God. God's creation was good and he handed it over to Adam in perfect condition. Adam failed in his responsibility and so God changed the conditions for his steward - but did not cancel the responsibility! Adam's task was made more difficult because of his sin but he was not removed as God's steward.

Adam's appointment as God's steward was passed on to his children and so down the ages to all humanity. Every person has a responsibility for the wellbeing of planet Earth. It is in our own best interest to care for our environment. There is a specific line of responsibility that passes on from Adam to all people, then to a specific nation, the Israelites, and so to the new Israel, the Church. Graphically it looks like this:

Moses

The momentous event that set the Jews apart from all the nations around them occurred in a desert while they were refugees on the run from a foreign dictator who had enslaved them to fulfil his grandiose plans to build an empire. Does this sound far-fetched? Or maybe it sounds all too familiar. God spoke to Moses, their leader, and gave them a code that is still the cornerstone of moral teaching and conduct for a major part of the world's population. It is somewhat battered and bruised as the result of attacks from every quarter but the importance of the Ten Commandments remains - for righteousness still exalts a nation (Proverbs 14: 34). And the dishonest scales of the modern business world can, even in the third millennium, bring nations to its knees - consider the problems faced by some of the industrial tigers in recent years. Starting with the Enron scandal the subsequent fallout in the banking sector has had a worldwide impact on stock exchanges. And corrupt practices continue to plague the world's economy and much of it due to a lack of responsibility and accountability and the dispensing of rewards to those who don't deserve them.

Moses and the Jews recognised that they were stewards. It was not their Law; it was God's Law. He was the author and they were given the Ten Commandments for their own good. They had the responsibility of obeying the Law and also of proclaiming it to the nations. So important was this relationship that it was established on the basis of a covenant. 'Now if you obey me fully and keep my covenant, then out of all nations you will be my treasured possession. Although the whole earth is mine, you will be for me a kingdom of priests and a holy nation' (Exodus 19: 5, 6).

The prophet Ezekiel proclaimed God's plan for the house of Israel after their failure as stewards of the Law.

'Therefore say to the house of Israel, "This is what the Sovereign Lord says: It is not for your sake, O house of Israel, that I am going to do these things, but for the sake of my holy

> name, which you have profaned among the nations where you
> have gone. I will show the holiness of my great name, which has
> been profaned among the nations, the name you have profaned
> among them. Then the nations will know that I am the Lord,
> declares the Sovereign Lord, when I show myself holy *through*
> *you* [my emphasis] before their eyes."' **Ezekiel 36: 22, 23**

The Israelites had failed but God was not finished with them for in the next verse he promises to restore them.

> 'For I will take you out of the nations; I will gather you from
> all the countries and bring you back into your own land. I will
> sprinkle clean water on you, and you will be clean; I will cleanse
> you from all your impurities and from all your idols. I will give
> you a new heart and put a new spirit in you; I will remove from
> you your heart of stone and give you a heart of flesh. And I will
> put my Spirit in you and move you to follow my decrees and be
> careful to keep my laws.' **Ezekiel 36: 24 - 27**

Christians have seen in these verses a prophecy that finds its fulfilment in the New Testament. So the responsibility for upholding the Law, while given to the Israelites in the first place and never rescinded, passes on to the Church. Graphically it looks like this:

Jesus

Jesus came as a steward and passed that responsibility on to his followers. As a steward he was commissioned to put into effect God's plan for the salvation of the world. He accepted that responsibility and even in the Garden of Gethsemane, knowing the price he would have to pay, he did not shrink back from his responsibility but prayed:

> 'Father, if you are willing, take this cup from me; yet not my will, but yours be done.' **Luke 22: 42**

Having died for our sins, Jesus was resurrected so that we might have the new, abundant life he promised. But the good news had to be passed on and so he commissioned his disciples:

> 'All authority in heaven and on earth has been given to me. Therefore go and make disciples of all nations baptising them in the name of the Father and of the Son and of the Holy Spirit, and teaching them to obey everything I have commanded you. And surely I will be with you always, to the very end of the age.' **Matthew 28: 18 - 20**

Christians are stewards of evangelism, stewards of the good news about the Lord Jesus Christ and his salvation. The Church is the result of the proclamation of the good news but is also the agent of evangelism and so is a self-perpetuating body. So Christians, by extension, are stewards of the Church. They form the Church but are also responsible for the Church. One day we will have to give account of our handling of that dual responsibility, for evangelism and for the Church. Our use of the word 'evangelism' from here on includes the Church. Please remember that evangelism and the Church are one responsibility. Clearly this is a uniquely Christian responsibility; it does not include the Jews or the world, as our drawing shows:

Our responsibility for evangelism is our primary responsibility and has a number of facets.

Firstly, evangelism is our priority. However, this does not imply that ethics and the earth are unimportant, as will be confirmed in the following chapters. It does mean that evangelism comes first on our agenda; that we do not preach a legalistic religion but offer good news, even though we may use man's inability to meet the requirements of ethics or his failure to care for the earth to lead people into a relationship with the Lord Jesus Christ.

In the second place it is our calling as Christians to care for the Church. This does involve our time, talents and treasure but they are the tools at our disposal, not our primary responsibility. In the past 'stewardship campaigns' emphasised the pledging of our gifts as our stewardship. Members were asked to make a commitment of a specific sum of money because of the needs of the congregation but without being made aware of their overall responsibility as stewards. This was putting the cart before the horse. It was misleading and dissipated the real emphasis of being a steward. The Church has suffered from the dubious benefits of the short-term gains at the expense of an awareness that the Church, the body of Christ, is the responsibility of every Christian.

We are stewards of the Church and we are to use all that we are and have to fulfil our responsibility - all our heart and soul and mind and strength. If we love the Lord then we must also love his Church - for he gave his life for it. One day we shall be called to give account of how we have exercised that responsibility for it is ours and ours alone. At the risk of being repetitive - we are either good stewards or bad stewards but we are all stewards.

Thirdly, God has given us all that we need to care for the Church. In all three areas (earth, ethics and evangelism) God is the owner/author and what he has done is good. The owner provides everything that the steward needs to do his job. In principle Christians have all the resources they need to fulfil their responsibilities! Yet the Church as a whole and many individual congregations are finding it increasingly difficult to meet their budgets, let alone capital needs or the challenges of mission and evangelism.

The problem is not a lack of resources - it is a lack of commitment and years of neglect of the Great Commission. And the lack of commitment is due, in part, to a lack of teaching. Christians have the resources but are not making them available.

In summary the three areas of a Christian's role as a steward are:

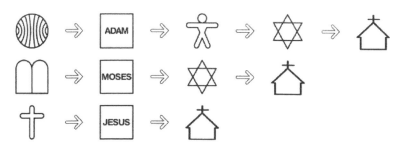

QUESTIONS

- On a scale of 1 to 10, indicate your awareness of your responsibility as a steward of the

  Earth   ......

  Ethics   ......

  Evangelism   ......

- How will this chapter change your prayer life?

- What changes do you plan to make in your attitude to God's creation, His Law and the spreading of the Gospel?

CHAPTER 5

Of saving acts and covenants

In the previous chapter we considered the three people who are the stewards that symbolise our three areas of responsibility. Adam was the first steward. The next major event in the Biblical story after Adam and Eve's sin and expulsion from the Garden of Eden occurs when 'The Lord saw how great man's wickedness on the earth had become, and that every inclination of the thoughts of his heart was only evil all the time ... But Noah found favour in the eyes of the Lord' (Genesis 6: 5, 8).

The account of the flood is found in Genesis chapters 6 - 9. For our purposes we focus on the fact that following the flood, God renewed the commission he gave to Adam with Noah and so Noah was appointed a steward of the earth. Genesis 9: 1-11 is the account and it is worthwhile comparing it with the creation narrative:

> Then God blessed Noah and his sons, saying to them, 'Be fruitful and increase in number and fill the earth. The fear and dread of you will fall upon all the beasts of the earth and all the birds of the air, upon every creature that moves along the ground, and upon all the fish of the sea; they are given into your hands. Everything that lives and moves will be food for you. Just as I gave you the green plants, now I give you everything.
>
> 'But you must not eat meat that has its lifeblood still in it. And for your lifeblood I will surely demand an accounting. I will demand an accounting from every animal. And from each man, too, I will demand an accounting for the life of his fellow man.
>
> > 'Whoever sheds the blood of man,
> > by man shall his blood be shed;
> > for in the image of God
> > has God made man.

> As for you, be fruitful and increase in number; multiply on the earth and increase upon it.'
>
> Then God said to Noah and to his sons with him: 'I now establish my covenant with you and with your descendants after you and with every living creature that was with you - the birds, the livestock and all the wild animals, all those that came out of the ark with you - every living creature on earth. I establish my covenant with you: Never again will all life be cut off by the waters of a flood; never again will there be a flood to destroy the earth.'

Before the flood God *promised* his covenant (Genesis 6:18), followed by the destruction of all life on the earth *except for Noah and those in the ark* - to allow for a fresh beginning after the flood. In response Noah, after the waters have receded, built an altar to *sacrifice* to God to show his gratitude, and so God established his *covenant* with Noah and his sons and all their descendants.

The following pattern emerges:

PROMISE -
    SAVING ACT -
        SACRIFICE -
            COVENANT

This is a sequence, which is repeated in the other areas in which we are stewards.

God promised to bring Moses and the Israelites out of bondage in Egypt and to establish them as his people. The promise was fulfilled, Pharaoh and his army drowned in the Reed Sea but the Israelites were saved, they built an altar and then the covenant was established.

God promised salvation to his people in the Old Testament, Jesus came as our great high priest and redeemed us by offering himself, once for us all, the perfect sacrifice and thereby established a new covenant.

It is interesting that the act of salvation is linked to the nature of the stewardship. Noah and family were saved from the destruction of the earth and then given responsibility for it. Moses and the children of Israel were saved from a dictatorship based on slavery to be custodians of an ethical code that has become the cornerstone of modern democracy. We have been saved from eternal judgement by the death of the Son of Man so that we can offer life to the world.

Much could be written about this pattern of events. What is important is that this process of salvation and covenant highlights the importance of our role as stewards of the earth, ethics and evangelism. They are based on acts of God's grace and confirmed by covenants by which God binds himself to fulfilling his part of the agreement.

If God has gone to such lengths to establish my relationship with him as his steward then surely the 'steward' relationship is one of the most important I have as a Christian. After all it was the first relationship in all creation as it was the relationship that God established with Adam.

In the absence of the owner, the steward acts on his behalf. If I neglect my responsibility as his steward that diminishes God's influence in the world. In teaching his disciples, Jesus was looking ahead to the era of the Church, knowing that he would return to the Father. He left them to be his representatives and so went to great lengths in many parables to emphasise our role as stewards. It is one of the most prominent and persistent themes of his teaching ministry. Being a steward is not an optional extra; it is vital, it is integral to our very nature as Christians.

Every Christian can say:
I am God's steward, his representative on earth.

If I am God's representative, it is no wonder that he gives his Spirit to be in me so that he may be revealed through me. Jesus came as a faithful steward and all the fullness of the Spirit dwelt in him. As I step out in faith to be his steward so I know the Holy Spirit has been given to me to enable me to fulfil my calling.

In summary:

- If you are a Christian then you are a steward.

- Why am I a steward? Because I have inherited this relationship as a member of the human race, because I have been grafted into the nation of Israel, and because I have been adopted into the family of God.

- How was it accomplished? By the grace of God from first to last.

- What has secured my status as a steward? Three covenants by Almighty God, who cannot fail nor change for he cannot deny his very nature.

- When did I become a steward? When I was born again through the Spirit as a child of God.

- Where do I exercise my stewardship? In my home, my school, my work, my church, in my neighbourhood, in the world - I am a steward 24 hours a day wherever God has put me.

- Who appointed me a steward? God himself!

And if God is for us, who can be against us?

CHAPTER 6
Stewards of the Earth

God's love for the world

> For God so loved the world that he gave his one and only Son, that whoever believes in him shall not perish but have eternal life. **John 3: 16**

This is probably the best-known verse in the Bible and a summary of the message of all sixty-six books.

The question usually asked is, 'Who does God love?' but it should really be, 'What does God love?'

God loves the world. The Greek word is 'cosmos'. This is the 'created order', that which is 'decorated' by the hand of God. God loves all of it; from the furthest reaches of space to the very dust that he used to create life. One day all who believe in the Lord Jesus Christ will come into their full inheritance - the eternal life he promised and has provided and for that day:

> The creation waits with eager expectation for the sons of God to be revealed. For the creation was subjected to frustration, not by its own choice, but by the will of the one who subjected it, in hope that the creation itself will be liberated from its bondage to decay and brought into the glorious freedom of the children of God. **Romans 8: 18 - 21**

On that day:

> The wolf will live with the lamb,
>   the leopard will lie down with the goat,
> the calf and the lion and the yearling together,
>   and a little child will lead them.
>
> The cow will feed with the bear,
>   their young will lie down together,

> and the lion will eat straw like the ox.
> The infant will play near the hole of the cobra,
>   and the young child put his hand into the viper's nest.
> They will neither harm nor destroy
>   on all my holy mountain,
> for the earth will be full of the knowledge of the Lord
>   as the waters cover the sea.
>
> **Isaiah 11: 6 - 9**

God loves all of his creation, not just that which is made in his image. It belongs to him and he loves that which is his by creation as well as that which is his by redemption. For

> The earth is the Lord's, and everything in it,
>   the world, and all who live in it;
> for he founded it upon the seas
>   and established it upon the waters.
>
> **Psalm 24: 1, 2**

If the whole earth is the Lord's, what is the basis of our stewardship of the earth? In the book of Genesis we have a very clear picture of Adam as a steward. All the elements that were covered in Chapter 2 are to be found in the creation narrative. God is the creator and therefore has the authority to pass on the responsibility for his creation. Adam was not only given the responsibility but also the means to carry it out:

> Then God said, 'Let us make man in our image, in our likeness, and let them rule over the fish of the sea and the birds of the air, over the livestock, over all the earth, and over all the creatures that move along the ground.'
>
> So God created man in his own image, in the image of God he created him; male and female he created them.
>
> God blessed them and said to them, 'Be fruitful and increase in number; fill the earth and subdue it. Rule over the fish of the

sea and the birds of the air and over every living creature that moves on the ground.'

Then God said, 'I give you every seed-bearing plant on the face of the whole earth and every tree that has fruit with seed in it. They will be yours for food. And to all the beasts of the earth and all the birds of the air and all the creatures that move on the ground - everything that has breath of life in it - I give every green plant for food.' And it was so.

God saw all that he had made, and it was very good.

Genesis 1: 26 - 31

In this account God created the sea creatures, the birds and animals and then man and woman. He was pleased with his work and gave it his blessing (vv 22, 28) and the command to multiply and fill the earth. To mankind was given the responsibility of ruling over the fish, birds and animals (v 28).

In the second account of creation, we are told that 'The Lord God took the man and put him in the Garden of Eden to work it and take care of it' (Genesis 2: 15). And he brought the 'beasts of the field and the birds of the air' to Adam and Adam gave them names - signifying his dominion over them (Genesis 2: 19, 20). God appointed Adam as his steward.

When Adam and Eve broke God's rule and ate the fruit of the tree of the knowledge of good and evil they were held accountable and God then changed the basis of their stewardship so that they have to work hard, 'by the sweat of [their] brow', to fulfil their responsibility - the idyllic situation had changed. But even then God provided for their new situation - he made clothes for them.

The final reference to the earth in the Bible is the promise in Revelation 21:1, 'a new heaven and a new earth, for the first heaven and the first earth had passed away'. Will it be necessary for God to create a new earth because of the mess we have made of it? With a growing number of extinct and endangered species; the continuing pollution of the land, rivers and sea; the on-going destruction of the rain forests and the depletion of the ozone layer - is it any wonder that the Lord will have to re-create the earth! And, sad to say, this is the result of a modern, enlightened society, with the wonders of technology and scientific discovery in a world 'come of age.'

Christian responsibility

Christians, more than anyone else, should recognise that they are stewards of God's earth. Christians should be more 'green' than any other group. They should be taking the lead in preserving the planet, in protecting the environment. Sadly, this is seldom the case. Evangelicals, as in many areas of life, have done the least. Nor should we throw in the towel just because of the enormity of the problem. Quite the reverse.

If the world has suffered it is often because we have not been stewards but exploiters - people who have not been concerned about the long-term implications of our actions, either as individuals, corporations or governments. Our greed has not been tempered by a holistic view - a view that should characterise the Christian approach. What can we do to meet our responsibility?

Firstly to go back to a basic principle. What God created was

- good
- beautiful
- in harmony.

We need to ensure that we reflect those same values - as individuals and as the Church. Only once we have done that have we earned the right to challenge the world about its stewardship of planet Earth.

Individual responsibility

How do we reflect those values as individuals? We must start with our lifestyle. Does it reflect the basic principles of creation?

Beauty, goodness and harmony?

It may seem silly or even trivial to some but if we are to start with our own responsibility as stewards of the earth, then we must ask ourselves the following questions. Firstly on a personal level: do I care for my home and garden and keep my car clean and serviced so that it does not leak oil or emit excessive exhaust fumes? Am I careless about litter, do I use environmentally friendly products, am I conserving our natural resources?

Responsibility as a citizen

Secondly, as a citizen, am I actively involved in conservation groups, using my influence in my business or company, lobbying my MP and local authority? Christians need to speak up and make a stand. Can you present the case for the Christian view of the environment and argue its merits? Christians need to be informed if they are to be effective!

Responsibility as a church member

The third consideration is the Church - in the first instance in its visible form, the building on the street corner. Many churches have a foundation stone that declares that the building was 'Erected to the glory of God'. Sadly, the glory has faded and the stonework is so dirty that it cannot be read. One of the legacies of the mediaeval age in Europe is its architecture - expressed in cathedrals, abbeys and churches. These beautiful buildings symbolised the goodness and greatness of God and often through paintings, sculpture and glass were in themselves a declaration of the Gospel. Dirty, dilapidated churches are a poor witness and it is no wonder that people stay away. It will cost money and time and regular work parties to ensure that our churches continue to reflect God's glory and beauty. And not only the building but also the churchyard - an overgrown garden and neglected tombstones are a poor testimony. And there are the positive things we can do as well. Putting flowers inside the church and planting them in the garden are ways of expressing the beauty of creation.

But the Church must also get involved in the environmental issues that face the world. There is only so much that we can do as individuals but united we can command greater respect for the Christian cause. Christians are not meant to stand alone, we are part of a fellowship of believers with the same goal. We should form action groups to monitor environmental issues, and then in a constructive manner lobby for change. And in an age where violent means are increasingly being used to achieve an end we should remember the command in Exodus 23: 2, 'Do not follow the crowd in doing wrong'.

Hopefully, our common bond as stewards of the earth will unite Christians from local churches and provide an opportunity for us to make our stand as stewards; and, at the same time, to act as witnesses.

To review our position as stewards of the earth. We can readily accept that God has the authority and that we have been given the responsibility as stewards of his 'cosmos'. When one day we face the Lord Jesus we will have to give account of our management of his possessions. I fear that the Church has failed and failed miserably. We have been bad stewards. We are guilty on a number of counts. We have been too spiritual to worry about God's creation. In this sense we have been 'too heavenly minded to be of any earthly use'. Next, we have been too selfish as stewards. We have taken the command 'to subdue and rule' as an opportunity to exploit and pillage with no regard for the beauty, goodness and harmony of creation. We have also been too shortsighted to consider the implications of our actions. We are in too much of a hurry to get results because we are pressurised by the demands of the world.

CHAPTER 7
Stewards of ethics

Over three thousand years ago a band of refugees who had been enslaved in a foreign country emerged from a desert where they had been wandering about for forty years and claimed that there they had met the one true God, that he had chosen them to be his special people and had given them a moral code that was to be the basis for all of life. Had there been a television news team in the area it is just possible that they might have covered the story because they were amused by these mad, egotistical, deluded fanatics who had obviously had far too much sun.

It was not a very auspicious start and the bookmakers' odds on it lasting more than ten years would have been very good. But it did last, even though many of their neighbours despised and ridiculed them for their stand.

Mighty empires have come and gone but the Jews have acknowledged that they are kept by God and recognise that they are strongest when they are obedient to his Law.

That has not changed. And the world has had a love-hate relationship with the Law and its protagonists ever since. For the faithful Jews were the odd men out. They did not fit in because they would not compromise their position. The Church has faced a similar situation all through its history. Its stand on moral issues has brought it into direct confrontation with secular authorities time and time again and more so in recent years. And with the increase in the secularisation of society we can expect that the Church's prophetic role will be needed more and more.

Public opinion is like a pendulum; it swings back and forth, often from one extreme to another. The world goes from a period of respect for the ethical teachings of the Bible to a rejection of those principles. Then follows a period of moral decay while people experiment with the latest fad - cooked up in the minds of philosophers who claim to be modern and so able to relieve us of the burdens of our superstitious past. It has been said that the only lesson we learn from history is that we don't learn from history.

So it is appropriate to ask, in the third millennium, whether the Church should stand by the Law that Jesus so clearly endorsed. Are we the heirs of the Jews? Are we also stewards of the Law?

Remember our theory starts with Moses, and moves through him to the Jews and from them to the Church. The move to include the Church with the Jewish nation as stewards, as custodians of the Law, started with Jesus. He grafts the new branches into the vine. He commands his followers to be the salt of the earth.

Right at the very beginning of his ministry Jesus made a policy statement so as to ensure that there would be no confusion with regard to his position in relation to the Law.

> 'Do not think that I have come to abolish the Law or the prophets; I have not come to abolish them but to fulfil them. I tell you the truth, until heaven and earth disappear, not the smallest letter, not the least stroke of a pen, will by any means disappear from the Law until everything is accomplished. Anyone who breaks one of the least of these commandments and teaches others to do the same will be called least in the kingdom of heaven, but whoever practices and teaches these commands will be called great in the kingdom of heaven. For I tell you that unless your righteousness surpasses that of the Pharisees and the teachers of the law, you will certainly not enter the kingdom of heaven.' **Matthew 5: 17 - 20**

And if anyone is in doubt as to the interpretation of these verses, let them read on from verse 21: Jesus does not give an easy option, a situation ethic that tones down the Law, rather the opposite. The commandment 'Do not murder' is linked with calling someone 'you fool', and anyone guilty of the latter 'will be in danger of the fire of hell'.

The apostle Paul sums up an argument on the Law by stating, 'So then, the law is holy, and the commandment is holy, righteous and good' (Romans 7: 12).

Christians recognise that they cannot get to heaven by keeping the Law but only by faith in the Son of God. But that is not the issue here. We are concerned with obedience to a moral code, which was given by God for the good of all creation. And Christians are stewards of that code, entrusted with observing it themselves and proclaiming it to the world.

In Proverbs 29: 18 we read, 'Where there is no revelation, the people cast off restraint; but blessed is he that keeps the law'. No revelation means no word from God, no prophecy, no guidance. In the musical *Fiddler on the Roof*, the main character, Reb Tevye says, 'Because of our [Jewish] tradition we know who we are and *what God expects of us*'.

In a world 'come of age' it is frightening that there are so many people who will admit that they don't know who they are and certainly don't know what God expects of them. But Western society is wary of authoritarian structures and with secularism as the god of this age it is not in a hurry to accept what it considers to be the 'restrictive' teachings of the Bible. How then will we win people over?

The short answer: by example. The long answer: by our example over a long time. This is the most effective method for convincing people of the validity of our case. If we fail to be an example then we are hypocrites and Paul points out in his letter to the Romans that this has implications, not only for God's people and the Gentiles, but also brings his name into disrepute.

> Now you, if you call yourself a Jew; if you rely on the law and brag about your relationship to God; if you know his will and approve of what is superior because you are instructed by the law; if you are convinced that you are a guide for the blind, a

light for those who are in the dark, an instructor of the foolish, a teacher of infants, because you have in the law the embodiment of knowledge and truth - you, then, who teach others, do you not teach yourself? You who preach against stealing, do you steal? You who say that people should not commit adultery, do you commit adultery? You who abhor idols, do you rob temples? You who brag about the law, do you dishonour God by breaking the law? As it is written: 'God's name is blasphemed among the Gentiles because of you.' **Romans 2: 17 - 24**

In the last verse Paul is quoting from Isaiah 52: 5 and Ezekiel 36: 22. The Jews had been given the Law and it was meant to shine forth as a beacon from Israel to the surrounding nations - their Gentile neighbours. In a style reminiscent of the Old Testament prophets, Paul is accusing the Jews of having failed as stewards of the Law with the result that their neighbours had taken to blaspheming God's name.

Substitute 'Christian' for 'Jew' and 'the world' for 'Gentiles' and read the passage again. We have as severe a condemnation of the Church as you will find anywhere.

The name of our Saviour - the name that is above every name and at which, one day, every knee shall bow and every tongue confess that Jesus Christ is Lord - that name is misused and abused on radio and television and in films, books, newspapers, magazines and general conversation every second of every day. Our spirits are hurt and offended by the callous insensitivity and arrogant indifference of the media and the public.

Are they at fault or are we?

Is God's name blasphemed among the nations because we have failed as stewards of the Law? Regrettably, we must accept some of the blame. The primary responsibility is ours as we have failed to set the right example to the world. When they see the Church dishonouring God's commandments and then imitate us they can hardly be blamed.

What can we do?

There is no short cut. In fact, we should be careful not to fall into the trap of our modern, pressurised society and seek an instant, quick fix solution.

We must set an example. We should be 'as wise as serpents and as innocent as doves' (Matthew 10: 16) when it comes to being the salt of the earth. When the Church is called on to make a statement about moral issues it should be a reflection of the Gospel, not simply in judgement but in evidencing the grace of God. We must acknowledge that we are sinners saved by grace and are therefore not standing in judgement on society but showing our concern for people, for society. But we cannot fudge the issue either. Many people are in a moral maze and looking for clear guidance on moral issues. So often so-called Church leaders are asked questions on the Church's view on an ethical problem. The reply usually is something like, 'The Church feels (or thinks) that this is a matter for private consideration.' There is no clear-cut answer; the water just gets muddier. Seldom is the distinction made between the Church's views on a subject and the clear teaching of Scripture. One despairs of hearing a clergyman point out that that the immoral practice that is being considered is clearly condemned by the Bible or specifically by the Lord Jesus and that what is being challenged is his authority.

When it comes to moral issues the Church stands before a watching world, with the media waiting to pounce on any Christian who breaks the rules. We should not expect anything less.

But Christians must not be passive and sit back and accept that a decline in moral standards is inevitable and nothing can be done about it. Fortunately Christians have not taken this view in the past or at present. An awakening has taken place. The silent majority is becoming more vocal. Christians are banding together. Letters are being written, complaints being made. And Christians are not alone.

There was growing concern in the nineties over the amount of violence in films and on television. In the first half of 1993 there developed something of a backlash against violence in films. National coverage was given to such names as Clint Eastwood, Jack Nicholson, Michael Caine and Sir Anthony Hopkins as they made statements of concern and regret about the level of violence in some of their own films. Christians have spoken up but so has an Orthodox Jew, Michael Medved, who took up the cause in his book *Hollywood vs. America* - thus fulfilling his role as a steward of ethics in a line that goes back to Moses.

There are three elements to our stewardship of ethics:

1. We have received God's standards for life
2. We are to be an example to the world by our ethical standards
3. In the application of our ethical standards we also proclaim God's grace and compassion.

Setting an example involves both teaching and living. The teaching takes place in the home and at church. We are an example both at home and through the church. But our example is to be seen in the world; our light must shine before men so that they see our good works and give glory to our heavenly Father (Matthew 5: 16). Christians should not be ashamed to promote their beliefs in society when so many modern theories have been tried and found wanting. Christians must also avoid a monastic mentality that views the world as an evil place and thus sees a need to isolate itself to avoid contamination. The trend towards 'Christian schools' can be a manifestation of this attitude. If all the Christian teachers and children were separated into Christian schools; who would be left to be the salt and light in all the other schools? Rather we are to go out into the world; into the classrooms, offices, factories, shops, the business and recreational centres of society.

We are God's representatives, the stewards of his law of life. If the Law is a tutor/supervisor to bring us to Christ (Galatians 3: 24); then as stewards of ethics we are doing more than upholding the

Law and being an example to the world; we are also pointing people to Christ. Being a steward of ethics is not in conflict with or a contradiction of being a steward of evangelism (the one of Law and the other of grace); the two are in harmony, the one enhances the other.

Ethics and Fundraising

There is also the question of ethics in fundraising, both inside and outside the Church. This is a separate subject but it is covered here as it fits in this chapter.

Our Priority: People or Buildings?

Christians have a steward's responsibility for the maintenance of the ministry of their local church and beyond it to share in the worldwide mission of the Church. Unbelievers are unlikely to support evangelism but may give towards programmes of social care that benefit their community. In the church some of the methods used to raise money, sometimes from unbelievers, and particularly for items of capital expenditure, are an insult to the Gospel. Many are good fun; others are blatant gambling. But most side step the issue of asking the people of God to meet the needs of the Church of God. Many see bingo evenings, variety shows, dinners, coffee mornings, cake sales, fetes and sponsored walks, runs, sit-ins, swims and vicars abseiling down church towers as valid methods of raising funds. But they really detract from the Church's calling and belittle the Kingdom of God. Churches, like charities, and often following their example, are always coming up with new ideas for raising money and they become more bizarre each year. But there is only one way to raise money for the work of the Kingdom – and that is by every Christian accepting his or her responsibility as a steward. Then there will be no need for this plethora of fundraising events and the Church can get on with its real work.

There are other needs that some churches face – particularly in the UK where many churches have been made Listed Buildings to protect them, as they are part of our national heritage. Often these churches and cathedrals have an importance because of their architecture, their history, and their music ministry. They get hundreds of thousands of visitors a year, both tourists and pilgrims. Many of the churches have small, ageing congregations that find the cost of maintaining the church prohibitive. What is to be done with these churches and cathedrals? Is it a legitimate ministry to spend huge amounts of money to keep open a tourist attraction, a relic of a bygone age? Understandably some cathedrals charge or ask for a specific gift from tourists. English Heritage and the Heritage Lottery Fund recognise their responsibility to assist with the upkeep of these buildings but the money available is a drop in the ocean of what is needed. Some churches will not apply for Lottery grants as they see the Lottery as a form of gambling. And even if there were pots of money available do we want to spend it on buildings that have little benefit to the church when Christians around the world are starving? We must always keep in mind the fact that the Church is made up of people not its buildings! To value bricks and mortar above people must be wrong. Some hard decisions will have to be faced. There are churches in villages with a congregation of ten or less and often one minister looking after five or more churches. People will get in a car to visit a supermarket but expect to walk to church. The wisdom of keeping churches open to satisfy a few when there are far more important issues facing the church is questionable. But it is a very controversial subject and few are prepared to face up to the reality of the situation.

Ethical Fundraising

Fundraising, as a profession, has had its fair share of unscrupulous, fly-by-night operators. Their misdemeanours get into the press (and a few culprits get into gaol) and fundraising gets a bad name. Unfortunately, the charities involved also suffer, even if they are the innocent victims. Donations fall off as public confidence in the charity declines.

If a charity is considering using a consultant to assist with a campaign then it is a good idea to use someone who is a member of the Institute of Fundraising or its equivalent in your country. Check the consultant's record on other campaigns and ask for references.

There is, of course, a very important difference between a professional fundraiser and a fundraising consultant. A fundraiser is someone who goes out in the name of the charity and raises funds for the charity. A consultant does not himself raise funds but advises, trains and equips a team to do the work of fundraising.

Fundraisers and consultants should never work on a commission basis. Many of the organisations that represent the profession will not accept people as members if they work for a commission. The public often find this strange as they think it better to use someone whom they can pay on the basis of results. There have been instances where fundraisers operating on this basis have used unethical methods, as they know that the more they raise the more they get. Christians will accept that 'the workman is worthy of his hire' and so fundraisers should be paid in the same way as other professions such as accountants and solicitors - based on time and travel and competency.

Transparency in fundraising is crucial. Paul was concerned that the handling of a generous collection destined for the churches in Judea was administered properly.

> And we are sending along with him (i.e. Titus) the brother who is praised by all the churches for his service to the gospel. What is more he was chosen by the churches to accompany us as we carry the offering, which we administer in order to honour the Lord himself and to show our eagerness to help. We want to avoid any criticism of the way we administer this liberal gift. For we are taking pains to do what is right, not only in the eyes of the Lord but also in the eyes of men. **2 Corinthians 8: 18 – 21**

Paul and his companions were entrusted with a very large gift coming from the Macedonian churches and added to by the Corinthian church. He asked the Macedonians to chose a representative to accompany the party – someone who would be able to report back to the church that the money reached Jerusalem safely and intact. To do so would be honouring 'the Lord himself'. Paul makes it clear that this is his priority and he describes it in a very personal way! He is also keen to show that they want to help. All societies are blighted by corruption and bribery and this is no less true of Roman society. And so Paul is prepared to go to great lengths to avoid any criticism, 'taking pains to do what is right' so that the faith is not in any way tainted by any suggestion of mishandling of the gift. This applies to being blameless both in God's eyes and those of the secular world.

Money given to the Lord's work must be used for that purpose alone. And when some use it to buy flashy cars, expensive suits and grand homes they must accept two things. Firstly that they will come in for criticism from the world and so bring the gospel into disrepute and secondly they will one day have to give an account to the Lord of what they have done with money given for his service.

CHAPTER 8
Stewards of evangelism

What is our premise in this chapter? That Jesus is the Gospel, and evangelism is the third area in which all Christians are stewards. And so how do we come to this conclusion?

We have seen that the Lord Jesus Christ gave the command to his disciples to go out into all the world and make more disciples through the preaching of the Gospel. The preaching of the gospel is the means by which the Church was established and on which its continued existence depends. The Gospel is God's great gift of forgiveness and new life through his Son and the renewing power through his indwelling Spirit. Without these gifts there is no evangelism and consequently no Church.

Jesus gave his disciples the command known as the Great Commission, a steward's responsibility for evangelism and so for the Church. By extension every Christian is a steward of evangelism, responsible for the proclamation of the Gospel. The steward's relationship follows the pattern established in Chapter 2: authority, responsibility, accountability and reward. We need to look again at the Great Commission to see how this works.

> Then Jesus came to them (the disciples) and said, 'All authority in heaven and on earth has been given to me. Therefore go and make disciples of all nations, baptising them in the name of the Father and of the Son and of the Holy Spirit, and teaching them to obey everything I have commanded you. And surely I will be with you always, to the very end of the age.' **Matthew 28: 18-20**

It is common to quote the last three verses of Matthew's Gospel and not verses 16 and 17, but they are very informative as they set the scene for the Great Commission.

v16: Then the eleven disciples went to Galilee, to the mountain where Jesus had told them to go.

v17:   When they saw him, they worshipped him; but some doubted.

The disciples had gone to Galilee in obedience to the command of Jesus, as it was passed it on to them by the women at the tomb. Verse 17 is a most significant verse as it gives the setting and the disciples' reaction.

Firstly, they saw Jesus. They had seen him in the Upper Room but time and distance separated them from Jerusalem and now he was there, standing before them. Secondly, their reaction was to worship him. A person or community in worship is ready for the Great Commission. For in worshipping we acknowledge that Christ is Lord and so are ready to obey him. A question is justified here, 'If our worship (individual and corporate) has resulted in a decrease in evangelism, is there not a major flaw in our worship?' We must look to ourselves and our worship before we seek to win the world. Worship ought to inspire and excite us to witness otherwise it is self-centred and selfish and is in danger of ceasing to be worship. *I didn't enjoy the worship!*

But there was a second reaction by some of the disciples: 'some doubted'. This is an amazing but very comforting statement. Some of the group Jesus was addressing still doubted, even though they were faced with all the evidence that he was the resurrected Messiah. Jesus was prepared to commit the Gospel into the hands of eleven very ordinary men. Evangelism does not need a group of super-spiritual beings for it to succeed - only a handful of worshipping disciples. It was true on a mountainside in Galilee and is true in churches anywhere in the world today.

All *authority* resides in the Lord Jesus and on that basis he commands us to go in the name of the Father, the Son and the Holy Spirit, and he will be with us until the end of the age. Authority is not only handed over from the master to his stewards but also is shared in a new way - made possible by the indwelling of his Holy Spirit.

The disciples take on the *responsibility* of:

- making disciples of all nations
- baptising disciples in the name of Father, Son and Holy Spirit
- teaching disciples to obey all his commands (which clearly implies that they continue the process).

Our responsibility as stewards starts with evangelism but it encompasses the whole work of the Church. We are responsible for the nurture of new converts, bringing them into the local fellowship to receive the sacraments, for worship, for teaching and training, for pastoral ministry, for the recognition of their gifts and the development of those gifts in the ministry of the church. This responsibility starts with our local church but extends to our denomination or national body and to mission, both locally and overseas. Each one of us shares in this responsibility and it is ours and ours alone. It is not something in which non-Christians share.

One day, at the end of the age, we will have to *give account* of our actions as stewards of the evangelism. We have at our disposal all the gifts that we need to be successful. Jesus said, 'I will build my church, and the gates of Hades will not overcome it' (Matthew 16: 18). Jesus is painting a picture that would have been familiar to his hearers but is a little lost on us in the twenty-first century. The image is that of the siege of a fortified city. Jesus is saying that he will build an army who will attack the city of hell and the gates of that city will not be able to withstand the onslaught. God's army will be victorious. Unfortunately, translations and interpretations of this verse have given a picture of the Church as a city being attacked by Satan's hordes with the Christians huddled inside. This is wrong - we are on the victorious side - we are doing the attacking (or should be); but one would not always assume this by the state of the Church.

If we are on the winning side, if we do have the gifts of ministry, if the Holy Spirit is convicting 'the world of guilt in regard to sin and righteousness and judgement' (John 16: 8); then there is no reason why we should not get on with the job - for one day we will have to give an account as stewards of evangelism.

Before we can close this chapter we must be practical about what it means to be stewards of evangelism. So far we have dealt in theory and the theory states that there should be no needs within the Church because God has supplied all that the Church needs to fulfil its calling. However, the Church finds itself in a very different situation, for it has a list of needs a mile long - and growing.

Amazingly, many churches in the western world, in the midst of an affluent society, are themselves poor. Of course, a shrinking Church will have a shrinking income. But the problem goes beyond that simple equation for the growth in wealth in countries in the western world has not always been matched by a growth in church income and resources.

The Church has the people, the people have the gifts and the gifts include the abilities and the money to do the job. We, the people of God, must release those gifts for his service so that we can fulfil our role as stewards of the Church. It will require a re-evaluation of our time, our talents and our treasure so that they are put at God's disposal.

The proposition looks like this:

Every Christian is a steward and every steward has been given gifts (time, talents and treasure).

The Church has needs and they must be met by the membership.

The equation is:

The gifts of all the Christians = The needs of all the Church

Or:

| Our time our talents and our treasure | = | The Church's responsibility for the earth, ethics and evangelism. |

This is a real equation, for what is on the left is equal to that on the right. If, therefore, the needs of the Church are not being met; then it is simply because

- not all Christians recognise that they are stewards or

- as stewards we are withholding our gifts.

The Church is sometimes accused of being 'so heavenly minded, that it is of no earthly use'. Is it not that we, the Church in the west, have been so influenced by the materialism of our age that we are so earthly minded that we are of no heavenly use? Are our priorities our own or those of our Lord?

Evangelism should be *the* priority of the Church. By definition the Church only grows through evangelism. Anything that has the potential to sidetrack us from the Great Commission should be tested and evaluated. If it is found to contribute to the growth of the Church then it has a place on our agenda. But we should be careful for many things appear beneficial but can divert us from our calling. In the sixties and seventies there was a lot of emphasis on the Second Coming. Many books were written on the subject. They often viewed the return of the Jews to the Promised Land as the fulfilment of prophecy concerning the last times. The Soviet Union was the Beast and Armageddon was just around the corner.

Jesus made it quite clear that no one knew the hour when the prophecies he had made would be fulfilled - even he did not know when the events they described would take place! Only the Father knew the date. This clear word from the Lord did not deter sincere Christians from writing book after book on the subject. One of the first, Hal Lindsey's *The Late Great Planet Earth*, was frequently used as an incentive to evangelise, but many of the following books involved Christians in a fruitless debate on the signs of the Second Coming. A lot of time, effort and money were wasted. Talents that stewards of evangelism could have spent more profitably. There are many other issues, very often spiritual ones that have been a diversion from our main task. Some are sacred cows and they are the most difficult to handle.

For example, revival would be perceived as a legitimate aspiration of the Church. Revival could be described as evangelism at an intensified level through an outpouring of the Holy Spirit. But we can be seduced into a state where we run around looking for revival and enquiring into evidence of revival without being involved in evangelism. Revival is a sovereign act of God in an outpouring of the Holy Spirit bringing conviction of sin, of righteousness and of judgement to come (John 16: 8). Historical evidence indicates that when it occurs there is no doubt as to what is happening. Unbelievers weep under conviction of sin; they often make public confession of their state; repentance and restitution are common occurrences; they desire to 'walk in the light as he is in the light' (1 John 1: 7). In recent times there have been so many new manifestations of spiritual gifts that it is right to enquire about their validity - especially when there is little or no biblical support for their existence. Paul's directive to the Thessalonians is still to be taken seriously.

> Do not put out the Spirit's fire; do not treat prophecies with contempt. Test everything. Hold on to the good. Avoid every kind of evil. **1 Thessalonians 5: 19 - 22**

And John had a similar warning.

> Dear friends, do not believe every spirit, but test the spirits to see whether they are from God, because many false prophets have gone out into the world. **1 John 4: 1**

The Church started with a revival on the day of Pentecost but the little evidence we have in the New Testament does not indicate that anything similar happened during that period. The apostles got on with the job of evangelism. Paul spent two years in Ephesus during which time he 'argued daily in the hall of Tyrannus ... so that all the residents of Asia heard the word of the Lord, both Jews and Greeks' (Acts 19: 9, 10).

So we should beware of becoming absorbed in looking for revival. Rather we should be praying for revival - until the Holy Spirit answers by blowing afresh through the Church to convert the lost. Until that happens evangelism is our primary, on-going task. God may send revival but the Great Commission is still our Lord's command to his disciples. We shall have to give account of our stewardship of evangelism and we cannot make the excuse that we were waiting and praying for revival.

CHAPTER 9

The theology and practice of giving

In over forty years in church-related fundraising, including thirty as a fundraising consultant working with charities involved with cancer, the blind, multiple sclerosis, schools, museums and hospices, I have regularly encountered the following statements:

'I couldn't get involved because fundraising is begging.'

'I wouldn't like your job as I can't ask others for money.'

If we are going to consider the Christian teaching about giving and that will have to include what is involved in getting people to give (fundraising) - then we can start with what they are not:

Not all giving is Christian and

Fundraising is not begging!

Beggars are people who have no money or resources. Fundraisers are (ought to be) people who have recognised a need and then have given of their own time, effort *and money* to help alleviate that need. In doing so they have earned the right to ask others to give. A basic principle of fundraising is that there is a lack of integrity in asking others for money if you have not given to the cause. No fundraiser can avoid the issue - time and effort alone are not enough - it is required of fundraisers that they set an example by giving financially to the cause they claim to support. And this applies to the trustees, Board members and leadership of charities and churches.

As the campaign manager for Bath Abbey 2000, a project to raise £2.5 million for the conservation and enhancement of Bath Abbey, my strategy was simply this; the Rector made the first Deed of Covenant (a tax enhancing, long-term gift now replaced by Gift Aid). He then challenged the members of the Parochial Church

Council; they gave with similar generosity and, in turn, challenged the congregation. Of the overall target, the congregation and Friends of Bath Abbey had their own target of £1 million and exceeded that by over £300,000. The Abbey is an important heritage and tourist attraction and so when the campaign team made their approaches to Bath City Council, trusts and businessmen they were not begging - far from it! In fact no other body equalled the generosity of individual members of the congregation, many of them gave sacrificially to the campaign. They were not beggars but people who could hold their heads high within their community. The final amount raised was £3.5 million.

Fundraising, properly understood and practised, is not begging. It is personal giving and asking others to give. These may sound like good arguments in support of fundraising but is there a biblical basis, is there a theology of giving? This is one of the most exciting things about being involved in fundraising within the Church - for there is a theology of giving - and it is near to the heart of God.

Giving as a reflection of the character of God

Christian giving has links with the doctrine of redemption as it is primarily a response to God's love as revealed in the cross of Christ but of course it goes back to the very nature of God:

You gave them this land you had sworn to give their forefathers, a land flowing with milk and honey. **Jeremiah 32: 22**

Every good and perfect gift is from above, coming down from the Father of heavenly lights, who does not change like shifting shadows. **James 1: 17**

'If you, then, though are evil, know how to give good gifts to your children, how much more will your Father in heaven give good gifts to those who ask him!' **Matthew 7: 11**

'Do not be afraid, little flock, for your father has been pleased to give you the kingdom.' **Luke 12: 32**

> He who did not spare his own Son, but gave him up for us all - how will he not also, along with him, graciously give us all things? **Romans 8: 32**

The thread through all these verses - and a thousand more besides - is simply this. It is God's nature to give - he cannot do otherwise. His gifts are good gifts, meant to build us up and make us more like his Son, that we might be conformed to his image.

When we give we are sharing in God's nature and surely there is no greater privilege for a Christian. This is proof that we are not conformed to this world and its most persistent and successful god, mammon.

Attitudes in giving

Giving should be the hallmark of Christians. However, the Lord is not only concerned about the gift but also the giver and the motivation behind the gift.

Firstly, we cannot offer gifts to God if we are at odds with our neighbour:

> 'Therefore, if you are offering your gift at the altar and there remember that your brother has something against you, leave your gift there in front of the altar. First go and be reconciled to your brother; then come and offer your gift.' **Matthew 5: 23, 24**

If we have wronged someone then God expects us to right the wrong before we can offer him our gifts. We cannot separate our worship of God from our relationship with our neighbour. Life is not divided up into separate little packages that are mutually exclusive. For the Christian all of life has a spiritual dimension, we cannot isolate one aspect and move it into another realm. God loves us and gave his Son 'while we were still sinners'; and he wants us to have the same unconditional love for his world.

Secondly, giving alone is not enough - how we give is also important. Paul sums up the Christian viewpoint when he says,

'God loves a cheerful giver' (2 Corinthians 9: 7) and this is because God is a cheerful giver. There is no credit in giving in itself, certainly not if it is done grudgingly or from guilt - it should be our joyful privilege. When Paul wrote to the Corinthians perhaps he had in mind an incident recounted by the Lord Jesus Christ of the Pharisee who boasted about his giving:

> 'The Pharisee stood up and prayed about himself; "God, I thank you that I am not like all other men - robbers, evildoers, adulterers - or even like this tax collector. I fast twice a week and give a tenth of all I get."' **Luke 18: 11, 12**

Here was a man who gave a full tithe and was, by his own account at least, righteous in fulfilling the Law. Yet he was trying to win God's favour - not giving cheerfully!

We must also 'give in love'. Paul warns us through his first letter to the Corinthians, 'If I give all I possess to the poor and surrender my body to the flames, but have not love, I gain nothing' (1 Corinthians 13: 3).

Early in the Sermon on the Mount the Lord condemned those who, while outwardly fulfilling the letter of the Law by giving alms, had failed in understanding the spirit of the steward's relationship. They had 'received their reward already' as they had sought the praise of men and so would receive nothing from their Father in heaven. Jesus went on, 'But when you give to the needy, do not let your left hand know what your right hand is doing, so that your giving may be in secret. Then your Father, who sees what is done in secret, will reward you' (Matthew 6: 3-4).

The command 'do not let your left hand know what your right hand is doing' is given so that we do not fall into the trap of the 'hypocrites'. In many church circles it has been used as a reason for a total silence on the subject of money. If in English society it is impolite to talk about money, so in churches in England in particular, the subject is almost taboo.

But the story of Ananias and Sapphira (Acts 5: 1 - 11) provides us with a sobering example of hypocritical giving. Verse 34 of the previous chapter sets the scene:

> There were no needy persons among [the believers]. For from time to time those who owned lands or houses sold them, brought the money from the sales and put it at the apostles' feet, and it was distributed to anyone as he had need. Joseph, a Levite from Cyprus, whom the apostles called Barnabas (which means Son of Encouragement), sold a field he owned and brought the money and put it at the apostles' feet. **Acts 4: 34 - 37**

There was no secrecy in these actions and there was no hypocrisy either! Ananias and Sapphira followed the example of others but with this important exception - they were hypocrites. They were quite entitled to keep all of the money as Peter makes clear in Acts 5: 4. Their sin was that they pretended to give it all when they had kept some back for themselves and they paid for their hypocrisy with their lives.

The meaning of names in the Bible is an interesting subject, and this is true of all of the people involved in this account. In fact Luke goes to the trouble of giving the meaning of Joseph's new name - the apostles call him Barnabas, which means 'Son of Encouragement'. Was he given this name because of his act of generosity in selling a field and giving the proceeds for the needy? The circumstantial evidence is strong for this supposition. On the other hand, Ananias means 'God is gracious' and Sapphira means 'Beautiful'. They did not live up to their names. God's graciousness was turned into something ugly.

This incident shows us that in the days following Pentecost the new converts made substantial gifts and they were not handed over in sealed envelopes. The practice appears to have been one of humbly giving to meet the needs of others in acts that were devoid of hypocrisy. If Joseph was given the name Barnabas because he had made a gift to the community, *perhaps it was in recognition of his generosity.*

Paul's letters to the Corinthians make the most amazing reading on the subject of giving. The sections in both letters should be read together. Paul boasts about the generosity of one church to encourage another church to give generously - far removed from the staid approach of many today! How then do we reconcile the words of the Lord Jesus Christ about giving in secret with the examples from the early church?

Firstly, Jesus' primary concern was with hypocrisy for it is a very serious sin. In the examples he used the hypocrites were seeking the praise of men and not of God. This is the reverse of the stewards' relationship - for stewards give account to God and not to men. If they seek the praise of men then they cut themselves off from receiving God's reward. Jesus used an extreme illustration to convey his warning that hypocrisy must be avoided at all costs: 'Do not let your left hand know what your right hand is doing' (Matthew 6: 3). This is reminiscent of his warning that 'if your right hand causes you to sin, cut it off and throw it away. It is better for you to lose one part of your body than for your whole body to go into hell' (Matthew 5: 30). Whilst it is obvious that Jesus did not intend his words to be taken literally, the vividness of his imagery indicates how strongly he felt. The context of Matthew chapter six is 'when you give to the needy'. This is a very specific situation and so we must be careful in using these verses to formulate a general theology of giving to the Church.

So what is the difference between Ananias and Sapphira and Barnabas and the others who gave the proceeds of the sale of homes and fields to the apostles? Clearly the latter sought no reward for themselves. Filled with the love of Jesus and prompted by the Holy Spirit, they gave because of the need and without seeking any glory for themselves. There was no hypocrisy in their giving. And because they sought no reward from men, the recognition they received from the apostles was not counted as a reward. They did what was expected of them. The same principle applies to the servant who, when he came in from the fields with his master, first waited on his master and then looked to his own needs. The master did not commend him for this as he was only doing what was his duty (Luke 17: 7 - 10). In the list of gifts in Romans 12, Paul encourages his readers to use their gifts according to the grace given them: 'if it is contributing to the needs of others, let him give generously' (Romans 12: 8). There is no merit in using the gifts God has given us. We have not earned them, they are not given on the basis of our spirituality - they are his gifts, given by grace through faith. The wealthy man who makes a generous contribution to the church is only doing what is expected of him, it is his responsibility as a steward in Christ's service.

Giving is important, but giving without hypocrisy is essential.

Of course it is possible to give in secret and still be a hypocrite. It is not only by outward acts that a person is a hypocrite. Hypocrisy is far more subtle than that; hypocrisy is a thing of the heart.

Take the standard practice in most churches. Giving is usually very carefully controlled so as to ensure that the confidentiality of the giver and the amount given is respected. Matthew 6: 3 - 4 is usually the reason for this practice.

But confidentiality is not the problem. The problem is that there are always people who hide behind the system. People who have not faced up to their responsibility as stewards but who want to give the appearance of being generous - they are being hypocritical. They are the equivalent today of Ananias and Sapphira. They may not literally drop dead in a Sunday service but they are in danger of an equally fatal disease - the slow spiritual decay that leads to death.

What we give is a personal matter between us and the Lord. He knows us and is never fooled. As individuals and as churches we must be very careful about pleading poverty if we are rich.

Most campaigns to increase giving in a church usually culminate in a Dedication Service when pledges, in sealed envelopes, are handed in, sometimes as part of the offering. This is a very solemn occasion calling for proper preparation of the congregation by the minister. The commitment is not primarily to the church but to the Lord and through him to the church. It is a time when we commit our pledges and rededicate our lives to him and his service. Such a service can be very meaningful and there should be a place for one in every church calendar. The Covenant Service in the Methodist Church is a fine example. As early as 1747 John Wesley recognised the need for an annual reaffirmation of one's faith. Many churches have followed the Methodist example, as it is a moving service. It follows a pattern established in the Old Testament.

How much should I give?

The next question is the most common one in fundraising, 'How much should I give?' There is a lot of confusion amongst Christians, even when the principles of Chapter 2 have been accepted. Many fall back on the tithe as the basis of giving. Then the debate begins on whether it is 10 per cent of gross or net income, and whether giving to other charitable causes is included in the tithe or separate.

Firstly, it must be said that giving as it is found in the Old Testament was not simply a matter of 10 per cent. The Israelites actually gave more and there were special 'capital projects', such as the building and rebuilding of the Temple that called for extra giving. Through the prophet Malachi God rebuked the people for not bringing the full tithe into the storehouse. God accuses the people of robbing him.

'Will a man rob God? Yet you rob me'.

But you ask, 'How do we rob you?'

'In tithes and offerings. You are under a curse - the whole nation of you-because you are robbing me. Bring the whole tithe into the storehouse, that there may be food in my house. **Malachi 3: 8 - 10**

Clearly there were tithes and offerings and the tithe had to be 'whole'. There were to be no short measures or inferior goods (there are clear warnings in Leviticus chapter 22 about unacceptable sacrifices). Malachi 3: 10 is a favourite text with preachers for substantiating the 'tithe' teaching. But tithing was the beginning of giving and not the end of it.

When Jesus spoke about tithing it was, in most cases, to accuse the Pharisees of complying with the legal requirements while ignoring the spirit of the law. Jesus was, therefore, pointing to a principle embodied in the Law that they had missed altogether. This is Principle 10 in Chapter 2, the principle of generosity.

But generosity is not easy to define. Jesus helps us when he says, 'From everyone who has been given much, *much will be demanded*; and from the one who has been entrusted with much, *much more will be asked*' (Luke 12: 48). Here he is laying out the principle which forms the basis of the modern taxation system, i.e. the more you earn, the more you are taxed. The tithe was not based on this system but on agricultural produce. While it pre-dates the occupation of the Promised Land, it was introduced in Israel's formative years after the allocation of land at a time when the people each had allotments of a similar size. It has an agricultural base and it is not clear how merchants paid their 'tithe'.

In Luke 12: 48 the principle goes beyond the basis of 10 per cent for everybody. Jesus is, in effect, saying that 10 per cent from a millionaire is not the same as 10 per cent from someone on a fraction of that income. For the purposes of illustration we can compare two families. The first is starting out with young children, a mortgage to pay and at the beginning of a career - small income and many commitments. In the other family the couple are approaching retirement, the house is paid for and the children have grown up and left home - maximum income and far fewer commitments. For the first family 10 per cent is a real sacrifice, but for the second it is only a small percentage of disposable income.

From his comments on the tithe Jesus appears to have considered it the basis of giving - but certainly not the upper limit!

Earlier in Luke 12 Jesus highlights the importance of our attitude to giving: 'For where your treasure is, there will your heart be' (v 34). The amazing thing is that he does not say, 'Where your heart is, there will your treasure be also.' Jesus was being very realistic; he knew the heart of man. Money plays a very important part in our lives and even if one's heart is in the right place it is no guarantee that one's money will follow suit. It is a verse for sober reflection as we ask ourselves the question: 'Where is my treasure?' C. S. Lewis had a knack of getting to the root of the matter, 'I do not believe one can settle how much we ought to give. I am afraid the only safe rule is to give more than we can spare' (Mere Christianity).

Giving to charities

Another question we must consider is: 'What about giving to charitable causes - is it part of my church giving?' Many Christians give to charitable causes that are not, in themselves, part of the Church. These charities care for animals, the sick, children, older people or for disaster situations caused by drought, floods or war. There are, however, many Christian charities doing similar work and most denominations have long-established programmes, both local and overseas. The Church is often poor at communicating with its members and it is not unusual for members to be unaware of this work. It is seldom as glamorous or dramatic as the stuff that makes media headlines, but as it is based on a long-term commitment it is usually far more effective in finding lasting solutions that are based in the local community.

The Church seldom gets good press and the world is largely oblivious of the work that goes on day in and day out within our local communities and around the world. The work that hits the headlines is frequently an immediate response to an urgent need and its emotional appeal encourages gifts to projects that may have no long-term commitment to the needs of a community.

As Christians we have a clear calling. The apostle Paul wrote to the Colossian Christians, 'And whatever you do, whether in word or deed, do it all in the name of the Lord Jesus, giving thanks to God the Father through him' (Colossians 3: 17). This is obviously an overall principle for Christian life. Everything we do is in Jesus' name. We do not take any glory to ourselves. In humility we acknowledge that he is the source of all that we have and are. We give him the glory in every aspect of life - especially when we make our gifts. This does not apply only to our giving in church but to all our giving. And it also means that the Church and Christian organisations are our first priority for they have the same goal. Many organisations are involved in 'good' works but it cannot be said of them that their purpose is to bring glory to God. Christians need to show great wisdom here for our purpose is the extension of the Kingdom of God - not that of organisations that have no interest in his Kingdom.

Wisdom is also needed as many charitable organisations are doing valuable work in terms of alleviating suffering of one kind or another and there are many Christians involved in this work. They are Christ's ambassadors and leaven in the dough. When Christians give to support such work we should make it clear that our gift is 'in the name of the Lord Jesus Christ'.

Giving in the worship of the church

And if there is a theology of giving then there should be a special place for giving in the worship of the church. The following reflects a practice that is dying out as many give by Banker's Order or Direct Debit but even when using these methods there is still place to acknowledge giving as a part of our worship.

The act of giving in most church services does not reflect its importance as an act of worship. It is that part of the service where Christians can express tangibly their gratitude to God for his goodness to us. Granted, we offer him praise and worship but there is nothing else quite like the act of giving where we can demonstrate our love for the Lord. It is a solemn privilege to share in the ministry of the church, through an act that confirms that we are stewards in

God's service. It is our confession that we long to show God's nature in our lives.

The act of giving should be a high point in our worship service; sadly it is usually the opposite. 'Taking up the offering' is one area that has been neglected in the renewal of worship in the Church, probably because people are embarrassed to talk about money or confused about its place in the life and worship of the church. Many churches get the offering over with as soon as possible or sing a 'suitable' hymn while it is being collected. Obviously, the leaders have forgotten what it is like to stand with a hymn book in one hand, your money or envelope in the other and then juggle with the plate while you are trying to concentrate on the words of the hymn. Hardly worship!

Surely there is no need to grapple with hymn books, collection plates, wallets, purses and envelopes while the offering is being collected? It would be just as appropriate to introduce a time of meditation and prayer and for the congregation to remain seated while the ushers pass the plates around. Then all can stand in an act of dedication of both the givers and their gifts and the offering is then placed on the altar or the communion table, in a symbolic act of commitment.

In the Presbyterian Church where I grew up, prayer preceded the offering. The ushers came forward and the prayer usually focused on the fact that we had given ourselves to God and our act of giving was confirmation of our commitment.

If there are a number of unbelievers in the congregation then it is appropriate to make the following announcement before the ushers go around with the collection plates:

> *We are now going to make our offerings to God as an indication of our commitment to him and his Church in this place and around the world. The members of this congregation have pledged their support for this work. If you are a visitor to this church you are our guest and*

so when the plate comes around please do not feel obliged to give anything unless you want to.

The other obvious link with the act of giving is with the act of receiving. In Communion we remember God's greatest gift - our Lord's sacrifice of his body and blood when we receive the bread and the wine. What better time to show our response to that love than in our act of giving? It helps us to focus on the truth that our giving is, in the first place, to God and not to the church. This is a very important principle as one hears all too often of people threatening to withhold their support of the church because they disagree with something that the church has done. Let them beware and reconsider for it may be that they are bargaining with God. Linking the act of giving with Communion also emphasises Principle 8 in Chapter 2: Christian giving is reciprocal giving. We give in response to God's many gifts to us.

Many churches are breaking new ground but generally speaking if there is an area in our worship services where there is a need for freshness it is in the act of giving and our prayers for the offering.

Motivation for giving

We began this chapter with the observation that *not all giving is Christian.* So within the subject matter of the chapter it is also necessary to consider the main motives for giving within Western society as Christians are faced with the need to respond to the ethical issues that can be raised. The three main areas of motivation are:

- philanthropy
- entertainment
- gambling.

There are times when they overlap but each area must be considered separately and we will start at the bottom of the list.

Gambling

Many people make 'gifts' to worthy causes on the basis of

gambling or games of chance. These range from national lotteries to a draw at the local school fete. Scratch cards, with the possibility of winning money on the spot; have become very popular in many countries. Many people participate in these schemes because they feel they are helping a charity and at the same time there is the chance that they will hit the jackpot. The Christian will have serious reservations about any fundraising practice that could be construed as gambling. But the effectiveness of this form of 'fundraising' should also be a cause for concern. National lotteries and scratch cards are bad news in terms of cost-effectiveness. At best 25 per cent of the money 'donated' ends up being given to charity. For every £1 given, 25p at most will go to charity – a seventy-five per cent cost ratio! The sums given to charity can be very large in national lotteries because millions of people are buying tickets. But for every £1,000,000 given to charity £3,000,000 has been swallowed up in administration, advertising, tax and prizes. It is quite common for the main prize to be far more than the amount given to charity. All sorts of people are making a lot of money through the administration and advertising of these schemes but 'donors' should be under no illusion - the bulk of their 'donation' is not going to charity. In fact, calling it a donation is misleading, as the name should surely reflect the primary destination of the money - which is not a charity's bank account!

In Britain many churches have spoken out against the National Lottery. The lottery's protagonists justify the method by the results but Christians must be very careful of a system where the end is justified by the means.

Entertainment

Entertainment is used to raise funds. Members of the public pay more for a ticket or entrance fee to an event than would normally be the case so that some of the money can go to a charity. In the UK this form of fundraising has reached epidemic proportions. The events are often useful for making the public aware of the charity's needs and so many have a valuable public relations dimension, but are they an effective and efficient method of fundraising?

Firstly it should be pointed out that, like raffles and lotteries, entertainment events rely on a large number of people making relatively small contributions. The numbers are smaller than in lotteries and the contributions are larger and so it is a more cost-effective way of fundraising than the gambling method. There are no prizes (or they are donated) and no or few paid professional staff and so that also improves the cost-effectiveness. Entertainers may need to be paid, however. In fact, many of the costs are hidden as volunteers do an enormous amount of work to organise the events. They are also heavily dependent on the media for free advertising to publicise the event. Newspapers, radio and television coverage is not free - someone must pay for it. Even major events that raise millions, such as telethons, would be sunk if they had to pay for the TV coverage.

It is difficult to put a figure on the cost-effectiveness of 'events' because it varies so much. Obviously, the more you use volunteers (who donate their time and skills and sometimes other things as well), the better the cost ratio will be. Many concerts, recitals and expensive banquets will have a cost ratio of 50 per cent at best.

The Christian is not presented with an ethical problem as with gambling, but charity events do go contrary to the biblical concept of percentage/generous giving, as it is common for everyone to pay the same amount for a ticket.

Fundraising consultants, in particular, dislike this method as it reduces everyone to the same level. The rich man, who can easily afford more, pays the same as the poor man for whom the cost of a ticket may be a sacrifice. The problem is also that the purchase of the ticket is deemed a donation to the charity and so a later approach for a straight donation can meet with the response: 'But I've already given.'

Philanthropy

Question: If it is love that makes the world go round then why is it necessary to offer prizes and entertainment before people will make a gift to a charitable cause? Or put another way: Where have all the philanthropists gone?

Everyone can be a philanthropist; your name doesn't have to be Rockefeller or Rothschild. One of the greatest gifts ever made is possibly that given by a widow who entered the Temple in Jerusalem over 1900 years ago and put 'two very small copper coins' into the box - it was all that she had (see Luke 21: 1-4).

Christians should give out of love - there is no other valid reason. The widow must have given to the Temple treasury out of love for God's house. Paul would reaffirm this truth when he wrote, 'If I give all I possess to the poor and surrender my body to the flames, but have not love, I gain nothing' (1 Corinthians 13: 3).

When people give to an organisation out of love and concern, because they believe that the work is worthy of support; then it is highly cost-effective and the bulk of the money is a donation and will help the charity. And in the UK a gift from a taxpayer to a registered charity will add 25% to the gift!

There will always be some cost involved in raising money as it requires communication with donors and the administration involved in receiving, banking and acknowledging their gifts. But the costs are kept to the minimum. It is not unusual for capital campaigns to have a cost ratio of below 10%.

Christians cannot use gambling as a means for fundraising. It is not much better if we have to resort to entertainment to get Christians to give to the cause. We have no choice, giving for a Christian must be philanthropic - but that is not the real starting place.

Theocentric giving

Christian giving is theocentric. Christian giving starts with God. He gave first - 'This is love: not that we loved God, but that he first loved us and sent his Son as an atoning sacrifice for our sins' (1 John 4: 10).

Christian giving is not primarily philanthropic; it is 'theocentric' it is done because God set the example through his love for us. Christians give because they recognise that God loves them to the extent that he was prepared to give his only Son for them - and we respond to that love. Christian giving is responsive or reciprocal giving. It is distinct from modern charitable giving where the charity makes the prospective donor aware of its needs and talks about giving the donor something in return. Christians should have a burning desire to give, even as God longs to give because that is his nature. Christians do not face the question, 'Should I give or not?' We are commanded to give. We also recognise that we give to the Lord through the Church. This is the first and main call on our giving.

Obviously, there is an overlap between philanthropic and theocentric giving. However, an atheist could be a philanthropist but not a theocentric giver. But a Christian is firstly a theocentric giver and consequently also a philanthropic giver. And this is a commandment from the Lord Jesus Christ:

'Love the Lord your God with all your heart and with all your soul and with all your strength and with all your mind, and *love your neighbour* as yourself.' **Luke 10: 27**

Most people involved in fundraising do it on behalf of others. They are not asking for themselves; they are a channel between the giver and the receiver. They are providing an opportunity for people to be charitable. In a more enlightened world the wealthy would not need prompting about their charitable responsibilities (always remember that wealth is relative). So fundraising is needed today as much as ever. Fundraising is a valuable and essential service in any community as no government is able to meet all the needs of society.

We close this chapter by considering some words of Jesus not recorded in the Gospels but quoted by Paul in his farewell to the elders of the church in Ephesus.

'Now I commit you to God and to the word of his grace,

which can build you up and give you an inheritance among all those who are sanctified. I have not coveted anyone's silver or gold or clothing. You yourselves know that these hands of mine have supplied my own needs and the needs of my companions. In everything I did, I showed you that by this kind of hard work we must help the weak, remembering the words the Lord Jesus himself said: "It is more blessed to give than to receive."'
Acts 20: 32 - 35

The Christian's attitude to possessions, work and giving are given:

- do not covet the wealth of others
- work to provide for yourself and to
- help those less fortunate than yourself.

Paul is saying that we should keep our eyes on those less fortunate than ourselves and not on those who are richer than us. It is like standing on a ladder. There are always richer people above us and poorer people below us. We must focus on those below us and who need our help and not worry about those above us as that leads to envy and covetousness.

Then Paul quotes Jesus as saying something that is the opposite of modern secular materialism where 'getting' is the goal of life. Jesus said, 'It is more blessed to give than to receive.' Most people get a great kick out of receiving a gift but Jesus claims that the one who gives derives greater benefit than the one who receives. If this is true it is because God enjoys giving more than he does receiving. The fact is: God is a cheerful giver.

CHAPTER 10

Demythologising giving in the church
or
Removing the fear of fundraising

A number of myths have grown up in the Church around the area of money and fundraising. We need to examine and challenge these, secure in the knowledge that here, as elsewhere, the truth will set us free to be effective.

For our purposes, a myth is a belief that has developed over a number of years to the point that it has been accepted as the norm. It has acquired a status that has elevated the myth to the level of the sacrosanct. It is difficult to challenge a myth because it is the received wisdom on the subject.

Myths develop from a number of sources. Some arise from experience - often bad experience. Perhaps the sermon on giving didn't result in a huge increase in giving. At the local ministers' fraternal church leaders hear of others with the same experience and the conclusion is soon reached that fundraising is difficult. Embarrassment over talking about money with members of the congregation adds to the problem and so the myth is established that 'fundraising is difficult'. This becomes the law of the Medes and Persians.

Myths also build up from a misunderstanding or poor interpretation of the Bible. These are the most serious kind of myths. They have incredible power for they are assumed to be biblical and in the hands of conservatives - evangelicals, charismatics and Pentecostals - can be a major problem. Such groups need to recognise the danger of becoming modern-day

Pharisees whose interpretation can take precedence over anything that may contradict it.

What are some of the myths that surround money, giving and fundraising in the Church?

Myth 1. Secrecy syndrome - Unbiblical to talk about money

The English don't like to talk about money. Some will go to extraordinary lengths to avoid a conversation on the subject and to get them to ask others to give to a charity is one of life's challenges as a fundraising consultant. A story from personal experience may help. I have met a British Army officer who was prepared to face 20,000 Russian tanks on the plains of Europe knowing he was vastly outnumbered rather than speak to another member of the same congregation in the same street about support for a project that they both recognised was desperately needed.

Christians can be like that. But they are far worse, or better, depending on your point of view. We have a biblical myth based on a very clear verse in the Sermon on the Mount. It is, perhaps, the most quoted verse on giving after 'God loves a cheerful giver'!

> 'Be careful not to do your 'acts of righteousness' before men, to be seen by them. If you do, you will have no reward from your Father in heaven.
>
> So when you give to the needy, do not announce it with trumpets, as the hypocrites do in the synagogues and on the streets, to be honoured by men. I tell you the truth, they have received their reward in full. But when you give to the needy, do not let your left hand know what your right hand is doing, so that your giving may be in secret. Then your Father, who sees what is done in secret, will reward you.' **Matthew 6: 1-4**

Regretfully, many Christians, both those in the pew and those in the pulpit, use this as an excuse for avoiding the subject of giving. Or they get very spiritual and tell you that 'it is between you and the Lord'. And of course it is - in the final analysis. But let us consider the text.

The words that tend to stick in the mind are, 'do not let your left hand know what your right hand is doing, so that your giving may be in secret'. That is where the myth begins. It goes like this.

'Giving is to be in secret. The Lord Jesus Christ was very clear on the subject. You will lose your eternal reward if you allow yourself to be honoured by men.'

The veil comes down and giving is consigned to a sort of holy of holies. *But have we not got our emphasis wrong?* Is this the right interpretation of the text or does it need further consideration in the light of the rest of the New Testament?

Firstly, the context is 'giving to the needy', not giving to the church. They are entirely different objects. So much of Christian giving from western churches to those in the third world can be demeaning to the recipients and can develop a culture of dependency. This is total contrary to the spirit of our Lord's teaching. Don't be trumpeters when you give to the needy. Poor people have dignity and it is often one of the few things that they still have left in this world. If they want to express their thanks for a gift then that is their prerogative; let them blow a trumpet in your honour but don't do it yourself. Remember, humility is a fruit of the Spirit; pride comes before a fall. There were times when I was in fulltime Christian work that financially we were very low. There were occasions when people left groceries at our front door. We were extremely grateful and asked the Lord to bless the givers. We were not embarrassed by the gifts and saw them as the Lord's provision in our time of need – but some people are and in some cultures and circumstances it can be very embarrassing. The Lord even provided us with a car through an unknown benefactor who sent the licence disc and third party insurance cover every year. Later we found that we had been a blessing to our benefactor though in a spiritual rather than a financial way. But when we get to heaven we will be able to thank people for their generosity in a way that is in keeping with the joyous spirit we will have in God's presence.

Secondly, giving to the church. We have already referred to the story of Ananias and his wife Sapphira; the couple who dropped dead at the feet of the apostles when they kept back money for themselves while pretending to give all to the church - it is found in Acts 5. The beginning of Acts 5 is, however, only the second half of the story which really begins at Acts 4: 32.

> All the believers were one in heart and mind. No one claimed that any of his possessions was his own, but they shared everything they had. With great power the apostles continued to testify to the resurrection of the Lord Jesus, and much grace was with them all. There were no needy persons among them. For from time to time those who owned lands or houses sold them, brought the money from the sales and put it at the apostles' feet, and it was distributed to anyone as he had need.
>
> Joseph, a Levite from Cyprus, whom the apostles called Barnabas (which means Son of Encouragement), sold a field he owned and brought the money and put it at the apostles' feet.
> **Acts 4: 32-37**

The believers were sharing their possessions, freely and openly. They did not claim them as their own. There were no *needy* people (the same word as used in Matthew 6: 14). The early Church was following the same practice as the synagogue.

Along came Joseph, a Levite from Cyprus. He sold a field and put the money at the apostles' feet. The apostles called him Barnabas, which means 'Son of Encouragement'. Did they do this because of his generosity? It seems likely as his Greek name is not a direct equivalent of his Hebrew name (Joseph means 'may he [God] add sons). Was this his new 'Christian' name?

What is very clear is that in the first church the believers were very open about their gifts. Nothing was done in secret. Gifts were laid at the apostles' feet - nothing was hidden - except by Ananias and Sapphira. In fact it is concealment (or partial concealment) that was their downfall.

At first glance the church appears to have been disregarding the command of the Lord Jesus Christ in the Sermon on the Mount to give in secret. The apostles could even have given someone a new name in recognition of his generosity. Had they gone directly against Jesus' teaching? This seems unlikely given their desire to acknowledge his lordship over their lives. Or would their understanding of Matthew 6 have been different from ours?

This is, I believe, the crux of the matter. The theme of the first half of Matthew 6 is hypocrisy in giving, praying and fasting. It is within the wider context of keeping the Law. Jesus used examples to emphasise that keeping the Law is impossible as we are sinners and transgression in one matter makes us guilty in all.

The Lord Jesus was vehement in his condemnation of hypocrisy throughout his ministry and so, understandably, used extreme examples in the areas of giving, praying and fasting - the three main areas of life in which the Pharisees were tainted by hypocrisy. Clearly, his illustration is not a prohibition on public prayer or otherwise we would never pray in public. As for giving - Jesus' primary concern was not secrecy but hypocrisy!

These incidents in Acts show that the early Church could give without hypocrisy and so secrecy was not the issue. But what of giving today?

It is fair to say that we give in secret - little sealed envelopes or by Direct Debit - but in so doing we may be hypocrites. For we can claim to love the Lord our God with all our heart, soul, mind and strength whilst keeping our purses well hidden because we are hypocrites when it comes to giving.

We face the very real danger of falling into the sin of Ananias and

Sapphira. Their sin was not that they kept back part of their money. Peter makes it clear that it was theirs to give or keep for themselves. The sin of Ananias and Sapphira was that they pretended to give everything when they had kept some of their money back for themselves. It was the sin of concealment that was, quite literally, their downfall.

Many churches and mainstream denominations are facing financial crisis. In the main they practise confidential schemes of giving. The level of giving in most of these churches is appalling, an embarrassment to the Church of God. Christians are making token gifts because they are putting God second in their lives. It suits them to use envelopes so that their giving can be kept secret and in so doing are proving themselves hypocrites - the very thing that Jesus warned against in the Sermon on the Mount! Secrecy is having the same effect as the boasting attitude that Jesus abhorred.

One of the sins of the Church today may be that of Ananias and Sapphira. People are not falling down and dying in an obvious way but the Church will still die if we persist in our sin.

This is, however, not a suggestion that we try to convince Christians that they must make a public declaration of their wealth and how much they are giving to the Lord – the Church has enough Pharisees already. But we must not be ashamed to speak up and preach about giving or let people hide behind Matthew 6 as an excuse for a total taboo on the subject. Paul wrote to Timothy:

'Command those who are rich in this present world not to be arrogant nor to put their hope in wealth, which is so uncertain, but to put their hope in God, who richly provides us with everything for our enjoyment. Command them to do good, (command them) to be rich in good deeds, and (command them) to be generous and willing to share. In this way they will lay up treasure for themselves as a firm foundation for the coming age, so that they may take hold of the life that is truly life.' **1 Timothy 6: 17 - 19**

Can you see young, timid Timothy approaching a wealthy businessman and 'commanding' him to be generous? I find it difficult but Paul obviously expected him to do it.

Giving without hypocrisy is our goal. But there is a secondary form of the secrecy myth that must be considered. In some Christian circles illustrations are used as examples of how giving in secret is honoured by God. George Muller of Bristol is a prime example. The China Inland Mission is another. Here are people or groups who never openly asked for support and yet were never short of funds as God supplied all their needs. These people are often held up as super spiritual and examples of how to be successful in meeting the needs of the Church. The conclusion drawn is that it must all be done in secret!

That it is God who supplies our needs I have no doubt. But I am equally convinced that it is not biblical to be silent about our needs. If it is then there are several pages from Paul's letters that we will have to tear out of our Bibles! If it is, then we may conclude that in fact Paul was decidedly unspiritual, as he was very forceful in urging the Corinthians to give. He did not want to be embarrassed nor for them to be embarrassed by their lack of generosity.

There is no need for me to write to you about this service to the saints. For I know of your eagerness to help, and I have been boasting about it to the Macedonians, telling them that since last year you in Achaia were ready to give; and your enthusiasm has stirred most of them to action. But I am sending the brothers in order that our boasting about you in this matter should not prove hollow, but that you may be ready, as I said you would be. For if any Macedonians come with me and find you unprepared, we - not to say anything about you - would be ashamed of having been so confident. So I thought it necessary to urge the brothers to visit you in advance and finish the arrangements for the generous gift you had promised. Then it will be ready as a generous gift, not as one grudgingly given. **2 Corinthians 9: 1 - 5**

It used to be quite common for preachers, particularly in missionary circles, to lay on Christians the burden of acting like George Muller - even if they did not realise what they were doing. If George Muller believed that was the way in which he had to trust God then that was fine for George Muller but it must not become a yoke around the necks of Christians today.

It is not biblical to be silent about the needs of the Church or about giving.

Myth 2. The Oliver Twist syndrome - Don't ask for more

Many people out of desperation may actually get around to asking for support for a church project, special need, missionary endeavour or planned giving campaign. But once that has been done they are dead against asking for more or asking a second time. They have the attitude that it is somehow wrong to ask someone for a second gift. It is as though once a person has given they are let off the hook when it comes to giving again.

In fundraising campaigns you will always get a few people who come forward with a donation without being asked. They will give way below the average and when asked to give again will quickly respond with, 'I've already given to the campaign!' - in other words: 'Don't ask for more.'

Christian giving, however, is a lifetime habit. In fact, it should continue after the grave - but more of that in a later chapter. Christians should never talk as though they have come to the end of their giving. On a number of occasions I have been told by sincere, dedicated, born-again, wealthy Christians that they tithe and that what I am asking them to do is obviously more than their tithe. It is as though they feel that they have met their obligation and so cannot be asked for more. If Christians question tithing it is usually for one of two reasons, firstly because they want to give a smaller percentage (in which case they try to discredit the tithe as the basis of giving), or if they are wealthy then the tithe is often used as a maximum (here they will endorse the tithe) so that they don't have to give more.

Christians can and should be willing to give to the Lord's work not only on a regular basis but also for special needs. There is a clear pattern of this in both the Old and New Testaments. Not only were the Israelites responsible for the welfare of the priests and the Temple but there were other calls on their giving for widows and orphans, and the capital projects for the building and maintenance of the Temple. David's plans for the building of the Temple are a wonderful step-by-step programme for a capital campaign, 1 Chronicles 28 and 29 have at least twenty specific points that you will find in any successful campaign.

But a more current example may help. In September 1991 I was appointed the Campaign Manager for a capital campaign called Bath Abbey 2000 to raise £2.5 million for conservation of Bath Abbey. The Abbey's congregation was our first target group. With the agreement of the Rector we set them and the Friends of Bath Abbey (who had £250,000 in the bank) a combined target of £1 million. We believed that they could ask for community support if they were prepared to set an example of generous giving.

When members of the congregation were approached it was made very clear to them that their gifts must not be at the expense of their regular planned giving. The Abbey is dedicated to St Peter and St Paul and members were not to rob the one to pay the other. The congregation responded generously. The average gift was just over £2,000 spread over five years by Deed of Covenant. It was not the wealthy residents of Bath who gave. Most of the active members of the congregation are schoolteachers or Ministry of Defence personnel or naval officers. By the end of the campaign the congregation and Friends of Bath Abbey had given over £1.1 million - the bulk of which was committed in the first year or so.

I went back to the Abbey as a member of staff in September 1992 to continue my work on the campaign. Early in 1993 the Bishop called the diocese to a new 'Giving Initiative'. Cutbacks in central finance meant that parishes were being asked to give more to planned giving. I was given the task of designing a planned-giving campaign to a congregation who had only twelve to eighteen months before given generously to Bath Abbey 2000. I developed the Luke 12: 34 Challenge on the basis of the campaigns I ran for Downes, Murray International in South Africa. The people at the Abbey increased their planned giving by 63 per cent. The average in the Diocese was 31 per cent.

But the story does not end here. I finished at the Abbey in 1995, by which time we had raised £2.7 million. In January 1996 it became apparent that with increased costs there would not be enough left over for the final project. As much as £1.6 million would be needed and there was only £150,000 in the bank.

The Abbey asked me to come back to help them raise some more money. And we went back to the same people. Most of their pledges had expired or were about to expire so we asked them to renew them. Not all did but the vast majority not only gave again but a good percentage increased the level of their gifts. I should add that since then the members of the congregation have been asked to review their planned giving commitments and every year it has gone up.

Why did this happen? Was it because they were all extremely wealthy and were only giving peanuts to start with? Certainly the level of giving increased dramatically from a fairly low level but the people involved were not millionaires.

Was there an exodus from the congregation? Quite the opposite. There was an increase in support and involvement (this is usually one of the benefits of a fundraising campaign).

There are many reasons for this willingness to give a second and third time. The two worth mentioning are example and results. Firstly, the example set by the leaders was a challenge to the rest of the congregation. Secondly, the members could see the tangible benefits that resulted from their support. While it can be dangerous and difficult to try to measure success in the Lord's work, in this case it was a bricks and mortar project and everyone could see that progress was being made.

A word of caution is needed here, as unfortunately there have been far too many cases of church and missionary organisations claiming success or conversions because they know that will generate support. This is more likely when there is little accountability to a Council of Trustees. Christians and the Church as a whole must be very careful that they can substantiate any claims made in their literature!

The Bible is clear. There is no end nor limit to our giving, just as there is no end or limit to God's giving.

Myth 3. Equality syndrome - Average Giving

So often one sees the concept of average giving being promoted by church leaders: 'If only we can get 1,000 people each to give £1,000 then we can raise a million pounds!' The 'average' gift appears to make us all equal. It sounds attractive as nobody is embarrassed by being asked to give more than the others. We are comfortable with 'average giving'.

Perhaps this myth stems from the idea that we are all created equal in the eyes of God. Equality in God's sight may be a reflection of our spiritual state but it is a great mistake to apply that to the rest of life. That we are all equal in God's sight is confirmed by the commandment given to Moses about atonement money. In between the instructions for making the altar of incense and the basin for washing comes the command regarding atonement money in Exodus 30.

> Then the Lord said to Moses, 'When you take a census of the Israelites to count them, each one must pay the Lord a ransom for his life at the time he is counted. Then no plague will come on them when you number them. Each one who crosses over to those already counted is to give a half shekel, according to the

sanctuary shekel, which weighs seventy gerahs. This half shekel is an offering to the Lord. All who cross over, those twenty years old or more, are to give an offering to the Lord. The rich are not to give more than a half shekel and the poor are not to give less when you make the offering to the Lord to atone for your lives. Receive the atonement money from the Israelites and use it for the service of the Tent of Meeting. It will be a memorial for the Israelites before the Lord, making atonement for your lives.'
Exodus 30: 11 - 16

The Lord gives equal value to the rich and the poor, both pay a half shekel as atonement money. This is a 'ransom' for one's life. It shows that we are all sinners who need to be saved. The Lord Jesus paid the final ransom at the cross. But this is very different from the concept of percentage giving, the tithe, which was the basis for giving in the Old Testament.

As regards our physical, mental, social and financial states - we are not created equal. We do not have the same height, IQ, social grouping or bank balance (or imbalance). In life we all have different incomes and different priorities when it comes to the disposal of our financial resources. It depends a lot on our responsibilities. It follows, therefore, that there can be no such thing as average giving. Why then do we persist in talking about average giving in the Church?

In the UK the Church of England has been facing a financial crisis for some time. There are a number of reasons for this situation but the bottom line is that for various historical reasons the people in the pew have not had to take the full responsibility for the day-to-day cost of running the church. The Church's assets in buildings and property and its portfolio of shares have cushioned the cost to the person in the pew. Also many parishes have reserves that can be £100,000 and more. For the person in the pew, most of whom don't have money in the bank, the request to give extra will likely fall on deaf ears. Giving in the Church of England is therefore lower than in other denominations - certainly those that don't have a similar portfolio of assets.

'Giving Insight' a report out in November 2011 is a survey into giving habits and practices in five denominations. They were Church of England, Church of Scotland, Church in Wales, Salvation Army and Scottish Episcopal Church. The survey reported that the average weekly giving in the Church of England was £9.77 according to parish finance returns. But across all five denominations the top 20% of people are giving £29.20 per week and this is 52% of the total giving. The bottom 20% give an average of £1.91 per week, only 3% of the total. So when a church calls for an increase in giving based on the overall average the top 20% are probably already giving far more and the bottom 20% see it as a massive increase that they can't afford.

In fundraising averaging the need is anathema! It is anathema for the following reasons:

I. There is no such thing as average giving. You can ascertain the average gift of a group of people on any particular day but that is an entirely different thing - it is static whereas giving is a dynamic activity with many variables.

2. There is no such thing as 100 per cent response. To talk of an increase in the average gift to a new higher level of average gift requires *everyone* that is currently giving to increase his or her gift. This is a 100 per cent response rate. If any Church got everyone to increase his or her gift, no matter the amount, then it would be the first fundraising campaign of its kind in the world to get a 100 per cent response. It just never happens in campaigns.

3. Asking people to give an average increase of say £x a week to a new average of £x+1 is a nonsense. If you are already giving more than the new rate then you could say, 'I'm doing better than that - let someone else give more.' The amounts quoted are trivial anyway and do nothing to challenge church members to give generously and liberally.

3. For families who are really battling, the average gift may be a discouragement. If you haven't a job and getting enough food for your family is a daily worry, then even the 'average' level may be unreasonable pressure.

How then should we present the need if exhortations to 'average' giving are wrong? Firstly, we must recognise that the Bible never talks in terms of average giving - and that should be enough warning. The Old Testament basis of giving is expressed as a percentage - the familiar tithe. However, whenever talk turns to the tithe, the questions start: Is it on net or gross salary? Are pension deductions legitimate? What about my savings? What are legitimate deductions?

The problem is that deciding on the tithe becomes a little bit like completing one's income tax return. It's a burden and totally contrary to the spirit of giving in the Bible - remember the cheerful giver? Then there are those who do not argue, they give 10 per cent. No more and no less. And they can be proud of it - inwardly of course. Again, this is not in the spirit of Scripture.

Zacchaeus is perhaps a good example of how we should approach giving. As a tax collector he had robbed the poor to give to his favourite charity - The Keep Zacchaeus Wealthy Charitable Foundation. This is the most common form of charity in existence and from it comes the oft quoted, 'Charity begins at home'. This is, of course, totally contrary to the Christian concept of charity - it starts outside the home!

When Zacchaeus encountered the Lord Jesus Christ he was radically changed. He was prepared to right the wrong he had done. And he was liberal in his restitution.

'Look, Lord! Here and now I give half my possessions to the poor, and if I have cheated anybody out of anything, I will pay back four times the amount.' **Luke 19: 8**

In calling Jesus, 'Lord', Zacchaeus was acknowledging a new relationship. He was no longer lord over his 'own' wealth but recognised that he had a new Lord who could command his loyalty. Zacchaeus presents a stark contrast to the rich ruler in Luke 18. The ruler had kept the letter of the Law 'since (he) was a boy'.

> When Jesus heard this, he said to him, 'You still lack one thing. Sell everything you have and give to the poor, and you will have treasure in heaven. Then come, follow me.'
>
> When he heard this, he became very sad, because he was a man of great wealth. **Luke 18: 22, 23**

How different: happy Zacchaeus and sad rich ruler. Zacchaeus knew he was a sinner, the ruler thought he was righteous. Zacchaeus knew he should be generous and that set him free. The ruler hung on to his possessions and was miserable. The name of Zacchaeus lives on, the ruler goes nameless into obscurity.

The writer of Ecclesiastes was also wrong. He thought that both the sinner and the saint would be forgotten after death. In Ecclesiastes 5 the Preacher bemoans that riches are meaningless. What is the purpose of being wealthy when so often neither you nor your children enjoy the benefits of your wealth? In contrast the story of Zacchaeus lives on as a testimony that God not only loves a cheerful giver but honours him as well.

Average giving is not enough; we must have the same attitude as Zacchaeus. If conversion to Christ does not radically change our attitude to giving then our conversion is shallow and even suspect. For if we have not been remoulded in this most fundamental area of our Christian experience, if Jesus is not Lord of our money, then what is there in us that has been converted?

The Macedonian churches set an example.

> And now, brothers, we want you to know about the grace that God has given the Macedonian churches. Out of the most severe trial, their overflowing joy and their extreme poverty welled up in rich generosity. For I testify that they gave as much as they

were able, and even beyond their ability. Entirely on their own, they urgently pleaded with us for the privilege of sharing in this service to the saints. And they did not do as we expected, but they gave themselves first to the Lord and then to us in keeping with God's will. **2 Corinthians 8: 1 – 5**

What a testimony to the Corinthians and to us!

Myth 4: Maximum syndrome - the tithe as the goal of giving

Under Myth 3 we encountered some of the problems associated with the tithe. Another very common problem is that in Christian circles the tithe has been elevated to be the goal of giving. It has attained mythical status. It has become the benchmark for Christians - do we tithe?

What was Jesus' attitude to tithing? In fact most of what the Lord had to say about the tithe was in judgement on those people who did tithe, who were extremely careful to ensure that they gave 10% of everything they had and usually boasted about their practice of tithing.

The Lord taught that a legalistic approach to the tithe was contrary to the whole spirit of the relationship between God and his people.

What did Jesus say about giving? Are we wrong to use the tithe as the goal of giving? Is there a New Testament teaching that replaces the tithe? What does the Church teach about giving and tithing?

I believe that the crux of our Lord's teaching is given in Luke 12: 48, 'From everyone who has been given much, much will be demanded; and from the one who has been entrusted (read 'steward') with much, much more will be asked'.

This verse is the basis of *proportional giving*. After nearly twenty years of looking for the organisation in the UK that evidences best practice as regards proportional giving I have finally found it!

The UK organisation that best evidences proportional giving is Her Majesty's Revenue & Customs Service. Income Tax is the winner. The more you earn the higher the tax rate. That is proportional giving. According to the Lord Jesus that is the way he views giving. A flat rate for everyone is not fair as the following examples show. They are based on salary earned in the 2010/2011-tax year:

Example 1

Income less tax less a tithe on gross income.

Income	Tax	Balance	Tithe	Balance
25,000	3,705 - 14.8%	21,295	2,500	18,795
50,000	9,930 - 19.9%	40,070	5,000	35,070
100,000	29,930 - 29.9%	70,070	10,000	60,070
	43,565		17,500	

It is far harder for the person on £25k pa to pay a tithe that for the higher earners. The top earner still has 3.2 times as much left after tax and tithe as the bottom earner. And the tithe totals £17,500.

Example 2

The only change is to replace the tithe with proportional giving, i.e. giving is at the same level as the income tax.

The top earner still has 2.3 times as much left after tax and proportional giving as the bottom earner. Proportional giving is £43,56 or 2.5 times the tithe!

Income	Tax	Balance	Proportional	Balance
25,000	3,705 - 14.8%	21,295	3,705	17,590
50,000	9,930 - 19.9%	40,070	9,930	30,140
100,000	29,930 - 29.9%	70,070	29,930	40,140
	43,565		43,565	

The examples show that even with proportional giving, higher earners are still comfortably off when compared with lower earners. It reminds one of the Lord's comments about the widow's gift to the temple treasury in Luke 21: 7

> As he looked up, Jesus saw the rich putting their gifts into the temple treasury. He also saw a poor widow put in two very small copper coins. "I tell you the truth," he said, "this poor widow has put in more than all the others. All these people gave their gifts out of their wealth; but she out of her poverty put in all she had to live on."

For people with wealth it is easy to tithe and I have come across a number who, with just a pinch of pride, have told me that they tithe, even double tithe.

Then there are the very wealthy who by moving their money off shore into tax havens don't pay any tax or very little. But when the Pharisees asked Jesus, 'Tell us then, what is your opinion? Is it right to pay taxes to Caesar or not?' He said to them, 'Give to Caesar what is Caesar's, and to God what is God's.' (Matthew 22: 21, Mark 20: 16 &17, Luke 20: 25). Clearly Jesus expected the Jews to pay taxes to the very system they hated. So it would seem biblical that wealthy Christians should pay their taxes the same as everyone else. And if they don't and yet benefit from living in the country then the implication is that others are paying their share towards the state coffers and so subsidising the wealthy!

I am not the first to advocate the concept of proportional giving. Ron Sider in 'Rich Christians in an age of hunger' has a similar system he calls 'The Graduated Tithe'. Sider's approach is from the imbalance that is illustrated in the title of his book. He writes:

> 'The graduated tithe is one of many models that can help break the materialistic stranglehold. It is not the only useful model, but it has proved helpful in our family. Certainly it is not a biblical norm to be prescribed legalistically for others.'

Rich Christians in an age of hunger page 187

The Graduated Tithe basically means that as your income increases so the percentage you give away increases. This grows until a point is reached where 100% of everything earned above that point is given away.

But I would disagree with Sider's comment that 'it is not a biblical norm to be prescribed legalistically for others.' I believe that the Lord Jesus does expect us to go beyond the tithe, that is the challenge of Luke 12: 48! But look again at the words Jesus uses in that verse and the verses that precedes it:

> That servant who knows his master's will and does not get ready or does not do what his master wants will be beaten with many blows. But the one who does not know and does things deserving punishment will be beaten with few blows. From everyone who has been given much, much will be demanded; and from the one who has been entrusted with much, much more will be asked'.

This is not a polite request along the lines of, 'It really would be most helpful if you could spare a few extra pounds to support a worthy cause'. Jesus's illustration is, quite frankly, brutal. It is in response to a question from Peter, 'Lord, are you telling this parable to us, or to everyone?' (Luke 12: 41). And the answer makes it clear that for those of us who know the master's will are the ones who will have to face the greater discipline, 'much, much will be demanded' and 'much, much more will be asked'.

And James is scathing in his comments about the rich:

> Now listen, you rich people, weep and wail because of the misery that is coming upon you. Your wealth has rotted, and moths have eaten your clothes. Your gold and silver have corroded. Their corrosion will testify against you and eat your flesh like fire. You have hoarded wealth in the last days. Look! The wages you failed to pay the workmen who mowed your fields are crying out against you. The cries of the harvesters have reached the ears of the Lord Almighty. You have lived in luxury and self-indulgence. You have fattened yourselves for the day of slaughter. You have condemned and murdered innocent men, who were not opposing you. **James 5: 1 – 6**

What he is saying is that wealth brings no benefit to the wealthy if it is hoarded, employees are exploited and it is used for personal luxury and self-indulgence. Is this a word against wealthy believers or the rich generally? Earlier in the letter in chapter 2 he refers to the preference given to a wealthy man who 'comes into your meeting'. So this could be an unbeliever but it certainly applies to the believer. James clearly believes that the gospel should impact the wealthy with a change of priorities when it comes to their use of their wealth.

Peter affirms this and makes clear the purpose of God's gifts, 'Each one should use whatever gift he has received to serve others, faithfully administering God's grace in its various forms' (1 Peter 4: 10). If God has been kind and enabled anyone to be blessed with riches then they are to be used to serve others.

Following the economic situation that started in 2008 the world is facing a time of austerity with many people unemployed or on reduced income. James speaks into our situation when he writes, 'Suppose a brother or sister is without clothes or daily food. If one of you says to him, "Go, I wish you well; keep warm and well fed," but does nothing about his physical needs, what good is it?' (James 2: 15 & 16). If Christians adopted proportional giving then how much more could be done to help those in need and what a testimony it would be to the world.

In 355 Julian was made Caesar. He was known as Julian the Apostate as he turned against the Church and reintroduced paganism in the Roman Empire. He is reputed to have said that to win back the people to paganism they would have to care for widows and orphans the way the Christians did. The Christians in the 4th century not only cared for their own orphans and widows but for those outside the church.

One of the best examples of generosity in giving is Rick Warren, pastor of the Saddleback Church in California, reportedly the eighth largest in the USA. Rick started the church from scratch and his books, The Purpose Driven Life and The Purpose Driven

Church became international best sellers. In 2005 Warren returned his 25 years of salary to the church and stopped taking a salary. He says he and his wife became "reverse tithers", giving away 90% of their income and living off 10%.

Myth 5: Selfish syndrome - Charity starts at home

Every week in the UK the national lottery has a first prize that can be as much as £10 million. Instant millionaires are made almost every week.

So many winners, when asked what they are going to do with the money say something like, 'We're going to buy a new house, a new car and have a wonderful holiday - after all "charity begins at home."'

As most of the winners already have a house and a car and have had a holiday within the last twelve months and what they propose spending on the 'new' ones is often a six- or even seven-figure sum, what do they mean by 'charity starts at home'? By Christian definition, charity starts outside the home. By definition, charity is the rich helping the needy. If you have a home you are not part of 'the needy'. If you want a bigger and better home that is another matter altogether. However, most lottery winners usually buy a home that they covet rather than what they need.

If you suddenly acquire great wealth you are no longer in need of charity. And if you don't have a home or a car and haven't had a holiday for some time and you need them, use your wealth to get them. But don't call it charity beginning at home.

What is charity?

Job in his distress remembered the good old days when he was honoured because of his charity.

> 'Whoever heard me spoke well of me,
>   and those who saw me commended me,
>   because I rescued the poor who cried for help,

> and the fatherless who had none to assist him.
> The man who was dying blessed me;
>   I made the widow's heart sing.
> I put on righteousness as my clothing;
>   justice was my robe and my turban.
> I was eyes to the blind
>   and feet to the lame.
> I was a father to the needy;
>   I took up the case of the stranger.
> I broke the fangs of the wicked
>   and snatched the victims from their teeth.'
> **Job 29: 11 - 17**

Job supported a wide range of charitable causes. They included:

the poor	the lame
orphans	the needy
the dying	the stranger
widows	the victims of oppression
the blind	

The range covers most of the charitable causes found today with a few notable exceptions. There is no mention of animals or the environment.

Animals were wealth in ancient times. One's cattle, camels, sheep and donkeys were a measure of one's wealth; Job started off with 7,000 sheep, 3,000 camels, 500 yoke of oxen and 500 donkeys 'he was the greatest man among all the people of the East' (Job 1: 3). Because livestock were wealth they were cared for. Just as we would not think of burning £10 notes, so the ancients would not mistreat their animals. The environment was unpolluted. Greenpeace was not needed.

Job's list has three main groupings:
- financial needs
- medical needs
- social and political needs.

The first four (the poor, orphans, the dying and widows) appear to be facing financial need. The poor clearly are in need, but orphans, the dying and widows do not have anyone to look after them - there are no workers to provide for them. Normally this would have been the responsibility of other members of the family but for some reason this practice had fallen down. Job stepped in to help.

Then there are the blind and the lame. Their disability probably meant that they could not work. Their need would continue into adulthood - it may have been a lifelong problem.

And finally Job is concerned for those who are not part of his society: the outsider, the alien, the minority ethnic group. These are the people who are easy to take advantage of, the ones you can pick on because they are strangers and it is easy to bully them. Job is prepared to take on the wicked amongst his own people for the sake of the oppressed outsider, the political refugee.

Job's involvement grows with each group. It appears that the first group needed financial help and not much else. But for those with medical problems, he became the solution - 'I was eyes ... and [I] was feet.' Job gives more than money for he gets personally involved.

In the last group he takes a protective role - 'I was a father to the needy; I took up the case of the stranger.' Job goes out on a limb for them, he opposes their oppressors and fights them to secure justice for their victims.

This is charity for Job, enabling those who cannot help themselves. It is linked with their inability to care for themselves because of financial, medical or political pressures beyond their control. Here we have guidelines for the Christian today, pointers to the causes we should be supporting, those in which the Church should be involved.

These are not new revelations. The Church has done more than any other organisation in meeting the charitable needs of its own members as well as those outside the body of Christ. We are commanded to love our neighbour as ourselves. And who is our neighbour? The Lord told a story of a Jew on the road to Jericho who was set upon by thieves. The only person who came to his aid was a hated Samaritan.

But note also that charity was extended to those in real need - those who, for legitimate reasons, could not work. Charity is not for those who will not work. Paul is very clear that this was the accepted practice, '... we gave you this rule: "If a man will not work, he shall not eat"' (2 Thessalonians 3: 10).

We have seen from the above examples and from the dictionary definition, that charity is the rich caring for the poor. And because they are not able to help themselves there is no stigma in receiving this help. But this means that charity does not include the arts or sport or heritage. From a Christian perspective these are not charitable functions in themselves.

CHAPTER 11
Legacies and bequests

There is an area of stewardship that merits special mention if we are serious about using all our gifts and talents in God's service.

In western countries legacies are the largest source of funding available to the Church. Potentially, legacies and bequests could revolutionise the mission of the Church. Legacies and bequests are not new; but they have been overlooked by the majority of Christians.

But before we consider the benefits of bequests it is edifying to see how bequests and the associated matters such as adoption and inheritance are used in the Bible to explain the nature of our salvation. The examples given in Scripture also point to a practice that Christians should follow. It is clear from the passages under consideration that it was the normal practice in biblical times for people to leave their worldly goods to their descendants.

> You are all sons of God through faith in Christ Jesus, for all of you who were baptised into Christ have been clothed with Christ. There is neither Jew nor Greek, slave nor free, male nor female, for you are all one in Christ Jesus. If you belong to Christ, then you are Abraham's seed, and heirs according to the promise. What I am saying is that as long as the heir is a child, he is no different from a slave, although he owns the whole estate. He is subject to guardians and trustees until the time set by his father. So also, when we were children, we were in slavery under the basic principles of the world. But when the time had fully come, God sent his Son, born of a woman, born under law, to redeem those under law, that we might receive the full rights of sons. Because you are sons, God sent the Spirit of his Son into our hearts, the Spirit who calls out, 'Abba, Father.' So you are no longer a slave, but a son; and since you are a son, God has made you an heir. **Galatians 3: 26 - 4: 7**

In these verses from his letter to the Galatians, the apostle Paul uses the following argument: before we came to Christ we were slaves 'under the basic principles of the world', but then Christ came and redeemed us from our slavery.

The picture was very familiar to his New Testament readers. Slaves are on sale in the marketplace. Along comes a buyer who purchases a slave by paying the redemption price, the cost of the slave. The slave then passes into the ownership of his new master.

Having been purchased by God we 'receive the full rights of sons ... So you are no longer a slave, but a son; and since you are a son, God has made you an heir.' Our heavenly Father purchases us to set us free, free to be *adopted* as his children. God cannot have slaves in his family for slaves do not share in the inheritance of the family and God has an inheritance waiting for us. This is a most amazing fact - God has made us his heirs!

According to Principle 8 in Chapter 2, Christian giving is reciprocal giving. If we give to the Church of Christ through a legacy in our will it is only because God has already made us his heirs, we already have a legacy from our heavenly Father.

When writing to the Ephesians, Paul says,

> In love [God] predestined us to be adopted as his sons through Jesus Christ, in accordance with his pleasure and will. **Ephesians 1: 5**

And to the Romans,

> The Spirit himself testifies with our spirit that we are God's children. Now if we are children, then we are heirs - heirs of God and co-heirs with Christ, if indeed we share in his suffering in order that we may also share in his glory. **Romans 8: 16, 17**

The reason that the Bible gives for God adopting us as his children is that he did it 'in love' and 'in accordance with his pleasure and will'. And now that we have been adopted we are not merely heirs but 'co-heirs with Christ'.

It would be futile to speculate on the implications for the Christian of being a co-heir with Christ in that place that he has gone to prepare for us (John 14: 2, 3) because we have 'shared in his suffering in order that we may also share in his glory'.

In the book of Hebrews we find something of the wonder of the New Testament teaching about our inheritance, as the Greek word for 'testament' or 'covenant' can also mean 'a will'.

> For this reason Christ is the mediator of a new covenant, that those who are called may receive the promised eternal inheritance - now that he has died as a ransom to set them free from the sins committed under the first covenant.
>
> In the case of a will, it is necessary to prove the death of the one who made it, because a will is in force only when somebody has died; it never takes effect while the one who made it is living. **Hebrews 9: 15 - 17**

Dying without a will is called dying intestate. The Lord Jesus Christ did not die intestate. He had no possessions of his own worth leaving in a will. On the cross he asked one of his disciples to take care of his mother – John 19: 26, 27 – 'From that time on, this disciple took her into his home'. There was no will drawn up by a solicitor, witnessed and sealed. But he did have a will – it was lodged with his Father in heaven. It was a new testament written in his blood. He had no earthly possessions to leave but left the world the greatest legacy it has ever known.

The Lord Jesus made a will that came into effect when he died, for in dying he paid the ransom price so that we could receive the promised eternal inheritance which is freedom from sin and adoption into the family of God and so become heirs of God.

When the Lord Jesus Christ died on the Cross his will came into effect. He died and in dying he left a legacy; abundant life now and eternal life in a new home in his kingdom of love, joy and peace.

What can we give as our legacy to his body, the Church?

Some practical considerations

What is a legacy or a bequest? A very simple definition is:

A final gift to a friend.

This is not a dictionary definition but it is helpful for our purpose. 'A final gift' implies that it is not the first gift but the culmination of a pattern of giving - possibly over a long period of time. It is the last one to be made. 'To a friend' implies someone we love, someone we care for - enough for him or her to be the recipients of our gifts over many years and of our final gift.

When a person draws up a will he is planning for the distribution of all that he owns to his friends after his death. This involves making gifts that will bring joy and happiness to his loved ones. He makes a list. His 'first' friends are his family, followed by life-long friends and then, very often, charitable causes that he has supported.

When a Christian draws up his will he must do the same. He must list his family and friends and that list should include his spiritual family. His spiritual 'home'; the place where he has been nurtured in the faith, where he has worshipped his Lord, where he has received comfort and support, where he has exercised his gifts, where he has shared in ministry and fellowship - this place called church - should be at the top of his list of 'friends'.

The Christian will start by making provision for his family. His wife and children will come first, although in many First World countries children are sometimes better off than their parents. Then there are also grandchildren to consider. Consideration of the immediate family follows the principle found in 1 Timothy 5: 8:

> If anyone does not provide for his relatives, and especially for his immediate family, he has denied the faith and is worse than an unbeliever.

Having dealt with that primary responsibility, the Christian should then be looking at ways in which he can make a meaningful contribution to the life of the Church through a bequest or legacy.

Development funds

In the first paragraph of this chapter it was stated that legacies could revolutionise the missionary work of the Church. It is my conviction, in the light of our responsibility for evangelism, that the bulk of legacies should be directed to support the work of the Church and to alleviate the suffering being experienced by our brothers and sisters in Christ around the world. Churches, dioceses, denominations should all have a Development Fund, with the specific purpose of funding this work - whether it be for a church on a new housing estate in our own country or for reaching out to an unevangelised group in a remote village on the other side of the world. Legacies and bequests would provide for:

- the training of clergy, missionaries, youth workers, medical and social workers
- the establishment of new churches, whether local or overseas
- the provision of evangelistic material, educational and social services
- the provision of food, clothing, medical assistance for those affected by natural disasters such as droughts and floods as well as those affected by the AIDS pandemic, malaria, TB and other diseases.

A Development Fund is best organised on a regional or national level but has to be implemented at congregational level. It is therefore appropriate that some of the legacy should be returned to the congregation as they put in some of the work to make it possible. This would be a percentage that is stated clearly in promotional material encouraging legacies and bequests.

Drawing up a will

Drawing up a will is a task for a solicitor. Dying intestate, i.e. without a will, causes a great deal of difficulty in finalising an estate and a lot of anguish to the family. It may result in your money going to the wrong people and a large portion going to the government. It is our responsibility as stewards of all that God has given us to ensure that we have a valid, up-to-date will.

It does not cost a lot to have a solicitor draw up a will unless it is very complicated. In 2012 in Great Britain a basic should cost between £100 and £200.

In many countries legacies and bequests to churches and registered charities raise the tax threshold on estates and in the UK this makes a considerable saving in what goes to the HMRC. Your solicitor will be able to give you advice on the best way of achieving the maximum for your beneficiaries.

'Would you be identified as a Christian by your will?' is the challenge to be found in an information pack put out by the Roman Catholic Church's Stewardship Department in America. Would you?

In the final analysis we must face the question; 'Is this money/property mine or is it entrusted to me by God to use to his glory?' If it is his and I recognise that he has freely given it to me and that I have been

> given a new birth into a living hope through the resurrection of Jesus Christ from the dead, and into an inheritance that can never perish, spoil or fade - kept in heaven for me, who through faith am shielded by God's power until the coming of the salvation that is ready to be revealed in the last time. **1 Peter 1: 3 - 5**

Then I make a last testament that glorifies God. And I do it cheerfully for I recognise that I have inherited something that I could never earn nor deserve. Many times in the New Testament we are told we 'inherit' eternal life, we 'inherit' the kingdom, we 'inherit' salvation. We inherit because the Lord Jesus Christ's legacy to his friends is that they may be with him to share his kingdom, his full and eternal life.

A Living Legacy

But do we have to wait until we are dead for God's work to

benefit from our legacy? Is there a way in which we can be generous both now and later?

I remember a conversation I had some years ago with a Christian in his seventies. I had given a talk on legacies and he wanted to know what he should do with his wealth that was largely tied up in the house he owned. He had bought the house forty years before and had paid a low five-figure sum but it had grown in value to a generous six-figure sum. He had two sons who both had well paid jobs and were not in need of a large inheritance. So, as he faced the prospect of having over £500,000 to give away, what should he do? We discussed the matter and he went away to do his estate planning.

My second story is more personal. Three years ago all three of our children were married and my wife and I were rattling around in a house that had four bedrooms and a small study. It was an eighties build so not a large house. I was self-employed and work dried up so we decided to downsize. We found a two-bedroom ground floor flat with a small garden in what had been a Council block of flats. We gave away some of our furniture to our children and had a huge spring clean to clear out an accumulation of things collected over the years.

Moving house, especially from one that has been the family home for decades, is a traumatic experience. As one gets older the tendency is to hang on to the memories of the past; and many of those are tied up in our home. Our move turned out to be very therapeutic. The flat needed a lot of work and my wife tackled the interior, with a little help from me; and I worked in the garden with a lot of direction from my wife. It very soon became 'our home'. We are very happy in our flat. It is a five-minute walk from our new spiritual home where God's people have been most welcoming and supportive. We no longer have a mortgage but also didn't have a huge profit on the sale of our previous house as the man in the first story would have if he sold his home.

But let's combine the two stories into one theoretical scenario that applies to many older Christians in the UK today. They live in large houses, usually with only one or two occupants, and with many rooms standing empty for most of the time. These houses are costly to maintain and heat. Unless there is a generous pension, some people may have to draw on savings to keep them going.

So what would happen if these people were to downsize? Some, if not all of the following would apply:

- there could be a sizeable difference between the money received from the sale of the large house and what is spent on a smaller house or flat,
- the cost of running the new home would be less and could result in a considerable saving each month,
- the move provides the opportunity to re-evaluate our possessions and pass on items we don't need to family and friends or give away to a furniture project,
- it may awaken an interest in the family's history as we uncover things we haven't looked at for years. This is a heritage we can then pass on to our children and grandchildren,
- and when we do die and go to be with the Lord we will have left our house in order.

The implications are that we will have a substantial capital sum, a reduction in monthly expenses and a property that will form the basis of our estate.

The capital sum may enable you to set up a charitable trust or just be very generous in giving to support the Lord's work. This should be discussed with an accountant or tax adviser to ensure your gifts can benefit from Gift Aid and the impact on death duties. By giving it away now you may save a considerable amount in death duties. Reduced monthly expenditure could mean that can increase your giving to the Church.

I can remember hearing that an elderly lady really enjoyed

making out her will as it meant she could give all her money away to the people and organisations she loved.

But there are some who could afford to give it away now and still have some left over to leave in their wills. After all this is not really our home, is it?

> Do not let your hearts be troubled. Trust in God, trust also in me. In my Father's house are many rooms; if it were not so, I would have told you. I am going there to prepare a place for you. And if I go and prepare a place for you, I will come back and take you to be with me that you also may be where I am.
> **John 14: 1-3**

CHAPTER 12

The church and its employees

If we work on the premise that all Christians are stewards; then the body of Christ, the Church, has the responsibility to do the Lord's work in his world. What happens when the Church, as an organisation, becomes an employer, so taking responsibility for its workers and calling on them to be accountable for their actions?

The diagram in Chapter 2 can be adapted for the employer/employee relationship:

Employer   delegates authority to the

employee   who accepts responsibility for a job within the organisation and must give account to the

employer   who pays the

employee   for his or her service.

In the model in Chapter 2 God provides his stewards with all the gifts that they need to fulfil their task. He cares for us and in spite of our failings still welcomes us into his house.

How does the Church compare?

It is unfortunately true that the Church, as an employer, has often had a poorer track record than many secular employers when it comes to taking care of its staff. This is perhaps not common knowledge as it is not something that is talked about. The Church can be very secretive about its failings. We are scared that this may reflect badly on God's ability to provide or his nature to be generous. Pride can get in the way of full and open disclosure of our failings and we want to present a picture of a victorious Church - not of our human frailty.

Very few Christian workers or clergy will talk about their conditions of employment outside their own circle. They are cautious about doing so as it may be taken as a hint that they are asking for more money. Or they fear that it may seem that they are stabbing their employers in the back and so putting the denomination or mission in a poor light.

Many Christians have a picture of working for a church or mission as a stress-free working environment where you are cocooned in spiritual cotton wool and protected from the harsh environment faced by those doing 'real' work in the outside world.

Working in a Christian organisation has its share of stress, disappointments and failures as well as the glorious confidence that as 'God is for us, who can be against us' (Romans 8: 31) and that he is at work in and through us to the glory of his name - but then that is just as true for Christians wherever their workplace.

Old Testament priests

In the Old Testament the priesthood was not considered as 'employment' in the modern sense but there are interesting parallels. Here was a group of people who did not earn their keep by working the fields or herding sheep - in fact it was forbidden for them to do so. They were set aside by God to provide a religious service on behalf of the rest of the Israelites. The tribe of Levi were assigned the priestly duties and so had no inheritance in the land. The other tribes were responsible for providing for the material needs of the priests. This is when the tithe was instituted. The other tribes gave a tenth of all the harvest and livestock and from these gifts the needs of the Levites were met.

> The Lord said to Aaron, 'You will have no inheritance in their land, nor will you have any share among them; I am your share and your inheritance among the Israelites.
>
> 'I give to the Levites all the tithes in Israel as their inheritance in return for the work they do while serving at the Tent of Meeting. From now on the Israelites must not go near the Tent of Meeting, or they will bear the consequences of their sin and

will die. It is the Levites who are to do the work at the Tent of Meeting and bear the responsibility for offences against it. This is a lasting ordinance for the generations to come. They will receive no inheritance among the Israelites. Instead, I give to the Levites as their inheritance the tithes that the Israelites present as an offering to the Lord. That is why I said concerning them: "They will have no inheritance among the Israelites."'

The Lord said to Moses, 'Speak to the Levites and say to them: "When you receive from the Israelites the tithe I give you as your inheritance, you must present a tenth of that tithe as the Lord's offering. Your offering will be reckoned to you as grain from the threshing floor or juice from the winepress. In this way you also will present an offering to the Lord from all the tithes you receive from the Israelites. From these tithes you must give the Lord's portion to Aaron the priest. You must present as the Lord's portion the best and the holiest part of everything given to you."'

'Say to the Levites: "When you present the best part, it will be reckoned to you as the product of the threshing floor or the winepress. You and your households may eat the rest of it anywhere, for it is your wages for your work at the Tent of Meeting. By presenting the best part of it you will not be guilty in this matter; then you will not defile the holy offerings of the Israelites, and you will not die."' **Numbers 18: 20 - 32**

The priests and the Levites had a responsibility to teach the Law and to offer sacrifices to the Lord. The people had a responsibility to look after the priests. And the priests also gave a tithe of what they received from the people.

Ministers and other church workers

The Lord Jesus Christ inaugurated a new priesthood and the old system of sacrifice is no longer needed. The Church is a 'royal priesthood' of all believers. The better sacrifice has been offered in 'the true tabernacle set up by the Lord, not by man' (Hebrews 8: 2). The writer goes on to say, 'By calling this covenant "new", he has made the first one obsolete; and what is obsolete and ageing will soon disappear' (Hebrews 8: 13). The Temple worship did disappear with the destruction of the Temple by the Romans in 73 AD.

The Church did not start with a new priesthood but the apostles fulfilled a teaching, evangelistic and prophetic role. It is apparent from the Acts of the Apostles that, in the main, they did not go back to fishing or tax collecting but devoted themselves to spreading the Gospel. The rest of the church supplied their needs. This is not the only pattern in the early church as Paul often worked at his craft of tent making with the express purpose of not being a burden to the believers. In 1 Corinthians 4: 12 Paul says of himself and the other apostles, 'We work hard with our own hands'. In 2 Corinthians 11: 8 he declares, 'I robbed other churches by receiving support from them so as to serve you. And when I was with you and needed something, I was not a burden to anyone, for the brothers who came from Macedonia supplied what I needed'. There is the suggestion that the apostles only resorted to working to meet their needs in unusual circumstances – when the local fellowship was not able to do so. Most of the time they were supported by the sending church or the churches they founded.

Ever since then the Church has had people in its service who do not earn their living by any other way than by being in the employ and therefore under the care of the Church. Initially, there were no employees in the modern sense but with the spread of the Gospel and the resultant growth of the Church a structure was established. The demands of the Church led to a more formal structure modelled to a certain extent on the Old Testament pattern. However, there are very clear differences. In the Old Testament the priesthood was hereditary whereas in the New Testament leadership was by appointment. There is no biblical evidence that elders or bishops were elected. Paul instructs Timothy to appoint elders based on very clear guidelines about their character and abilities.

The relationship between the Church and its 'employees' has taken many forms in situations ranging from monastic communities to independent churches. In the former the 'employee' receives little or no salary but all other needs are provided. In the extreme example of the latter the pastor may even determine his own salary. There is no need to look at the history of these relationships but the current situation is important for a number of reasons.

Church members are often ignorant about the salary the minister is receiving and dismayed when they find out – usually because it is so low. Few realise or recognise that they have a responsibility in this matter as they are, in one sense, the employers of the minister. Many Christians, particularly in evangelical circles, are also asked to support 'full-time' workers in missionary and parachurch organisations. This influences their giving and their support for their local church. And having been on the 'full-time' workers' side of the fence I know it is very important to them as well. But whereas there are structures in place in mainstream churches to regulate staff employment this is not always the case with some small missions and independent churches. If it is a stewardship relationship, who takes responsibility for the workers and to whom are they accountable? And how are they rewarded?

These are not questions that will go away or can be swept under the carpet. There is increasing pressure on fundraising. Both mainstream denominations and missionary organisations have to increase their income. Many are using a more professional approach.

The degree of support given to church workers, whatever the denomination or level of service, is often directly related to the way in which the church views its workers. In the Roman Catholic Church service is considered a vocation for life and so the Church accepts its responsibility to care for its clergy and nuns while they are alive. The level of care may vary but it is always there. Many other mainstream denominations have improved their salary structures but the provision for retirement is often inadequate. The missionary organisations quite often have the worst record of care. They may not have a long-term view of service. They don't have a church base but only the support, at a distance, of some church members who get their newsletter. Who provides for the missionary returning home after forty years' service in a developing country?

Then there is the question of furlough. For foreign-based missionaries the opportunity to return to their home country after a number of years in a foreign culture without the close support of friends and family is an exciting prospect. It is a time of refreshment, renewal, and relaxation. It is an opportunity to renew friendships and catch up with the family news. It is also a time to visit supporting churches and to establish contact with new supporters. All this must be done in a matter of months and often involves a lot of travelling. No wonder some missionaries are glad to be back on station as being on furlough is more exhausting than missionary work. It is especially difficult for those missionaries who have to raise their own support. They are under constant pressure to recruit new supporters and very often without any training in fundraising. Furlough is not a holiday for most missionaries.

Is it right to put missionaries through this process?

But what about ministers and 'fulltime' workers based at home? Do they get a remuneration that enables them to have a proper holiday? Why should they have to make do with second best when the rest of the congregation is flying to exotic destinations?

The Rights of an Apostle

In the New International Version the heading for 1 Corinthians 9 is The Rights of an Apostle. And the root of the Greek word apostle is 'to send' and missionary has the same root in Latin. If someone is sent then those who do the sending must take responsibility for the people they send. Paul says that those who are sent have rights. What are the rights of those who are sent out in the Lord's service?

> Don't we have the right to food and drink? Don't we have the right to take a believing wife along with us, as do the other apostles and the Lord's brothers and Cephas? Or is it only I and Barnabas who must work for a living?

Who serves as a soldier at his own expense? Who plants a vineyard and does not eat of its grapes? Who tends a flock and does not drink of the milk? Do I say this merely from a human point of view? Doesn't the Law say the same thing? For it is written in the Law of Moses: 'Do not muzzle an ox while it is treading out the grain.' Is it about oxen that God is concerned? Surely he says this for us, doesn't he? Yes, this was written for us, because when the ploughman ploughs and the thresher threshes, they ought to do so in the hope of sharing in the harvest. If we have sown spiritual seed among you, is it too much if we reap a material harvest from you? If others have this right of support from you, shouldn't we have it all the more?

But we did not use this right. On the contrary, we put up with anything rather than hinder the gospel of Christ. Don't you know that those who work in the temple get their food from the temple, and those who serve at the altar share in what is offered on the altar? In the same way, the Lord has commanded that those who preach the gospel should receive their living from the gospel. **1 Corinthians 9: 4 – 14**

There are thirteen questions in this passage and one answer: 'the Lord has *commanded* that those who preach the gospel should receive their living from the gospel'.

Paul goes on to explain why he didn't exercise his rights with the Corinthian church - *but that was his prerogative.* The fact remains that those who work for the Church are entitled to receive their living from the Church. The church or missionary society that expects its workers to raise their own support and also a proportion of the administration costs is adopting a practice that is questionable from a biblical perspective. It is passing on its responsibility to others, some of whom may be very successful while others find it to be a very heavy burden. It is obvious why it is done; supporters would much rather give to an individual they know than an organisation in an office far away. But it is extremely short sighted of the organisation for when a worker leaves the organisation their support usually goes with them especially if they are moving to another organisation. This applies not only to regular giving but also the potential for legacy income.

The bottom line is that the Church must take responsibility for its workers. The members of a church must ensure that their minister is being properly paid. And this includes the provision of a home and a pension. Some denominations and missionary organisations provide housing but not a home. When the worker retires he or she has no home and an inadequate pension. This is a grievous sin. It runs contrary to the whole concept of responsibility. Within the concept of the extended Christian family, 'If anyone does not provide for his relatives... he has denied the faith and is worse than an unbeliever' (1 Timothy 5: 8).

CHAPTER 13

Accountability and reward

Our basic premise on stewards involves a relationship that has four essential elements:

- authority
- responsibility
- accountability
- reward.

In the preceding chapters we have concentrated on the first two elements and hardly touched on the last two. Now we must consider these two equally important and awesome concepts: accountability and reward. They flow from God's authority and our responsibility.

God himself has given us authority to go out into the world as his stewards - we go in his name and with his power at our disposal. We accept our responsibility as stewards of the earth, ethics and evangelism. We are either good stewards or bad stewards - but we are always stewards.

Accountability

As stewards we are accountable to and rewarded by our heavenly Father.

The biblical picture of stewardship is very clear. Jesus, in his parables was clear. One day we must give account of how we have used our gifts in fulfilling that responsibility. It is not as though they are 'our' possessions, 'our' time, 'our' talents and 'our' treasure. They are God's gifts to be used in his service.

When do we give account?

The answer is both here and now and also in the future when, one day, we face our Lord. We give account as individuals on a daily basis as we meet with God in prayer, but there is a corporate church accountability as well.

Every year, at the annual general meeting (AGM) of the church, we should be giving account as stewards. The AGM of a church should not be a meeting just to present the audited accounts and to receive the reports of the various groups about what they have or have not done during the year. As anyone can tell you that is usually deadly boring stuff.

No! An AGM should be the time when before our Lord we review our progress compared with the vision he has given us and with the goals we have set, possibly under the headings: earth, ethics and evangelism. It should also be the time when we are encouraged, as individuals, to consider our own progress in the faith, to 'examine [y]ourselves to see whether we are in the faith; test [y]ourselves' (2 Corinthians 13: 5). Accountability is an individual matter in the first instance. Christians should make an annual review of their own standing before the Lord, and the time of the church's AGM is perhaps the appropriate time for a personal as well as a corporate review.

For a managing director in business, the AGM is a very serious matter for he must satisfy the shareholders that the company is being properly run. He must show a profit, give evidence that he is meeting the short and long-term goals of the Board, prove that the company is being run efficiently and has a satisfied workforce, and that he has plans for the future designed to meet changing market needs. If he has done all of this then the AGM is a happy occasion with much celebration; but if not, then it is doom and gloom, the share-price falls on the Stock Exchange and the managing director may be looking for a new job.

If churches were to take a similar approach (in a spirit of love) at their annual general meetings, keeping in mind the spiritual nature and priorities of the Church, it could bring in a breath of fresh air. If an AGM is merely a rubber stamp to maintain the status quo, to breathe a sigh of relief that we are still in the black (just), then we are not taking seriously the need to give an account of our responsibility as stewards.

The church's AGM may have to meet certain legal requirements such as the approval of the audited accounts and the appointment of professional services but it should be viewed as *our report to our Lord of our use of his gifts over the past year*. It is primarily a spiritual exercise; it is part of our worship; it is our acknowledgement that Jesus is our Lord and Lord of our church. Our agenda should be the spiritual values of the church and include an analysis of our growth in numbers and in depth, our impact on our society as light and salt, our ministry in caring for our community and our environment, and our plans to improve our ministry and meet new needs. Christ is building his Church according to his predetermined plan and we need to plan for our growth.

This exercise should be conducted at *local, regional and national level* depending on the size and nature of the organisation. It is the primary way in which we can be accountable as stewards. Even a cursory reading of Paul's letters to Timothy and Titus shows that Paul held them accountable for their ministry.

There is also another occasion on which we must give account - that day when we meet our Lord Jesus Christ face to face. We will have to give account as stewards reporting back to our Lord. How that works I do not know but I believe every Christian would want to hear Jesus say,

> 'Well done good and faithful servant! ... Come and share your master's happiness!' **Matthew 25: 21**

Reward

If accountability is a difficult subject then reward is even more so. Some people would view the concept of reward as a challenge to the doctrine of justification by faith. Their argument is:

We are unworthy sinners having no merit of our own. How then can we talk of our Lord rewarding us for works we have done when any goodness in us has been the result of the Spirit of God working out His plan and purpose in and through us? Reward appears to be a contradiction to justification by faith.

Yet we cannot escape the teaching of the Lord Jesus. Our Lord constantly referred to rewards and punishments when teaching the disciples.

In the Beatitudes Jesus promises his disciples that the result of their sacrifice for the Kingdom is that they should

> Rejoice in that day and leap for joy, because great is your reward in heaven. **Luke 6: 23**

The Lord goes on to say,

> ... love your enemies, do good to them, and lend to them without expecting to get anything back. Then your reward will be great, and you will be sons of the Most High, because he is kind to the ungrateful and wicked. Be merciful, just as your Father is merciful.' **Luke 6: 35, 36**

Of course there are different kinds of reward. On a personal level there is a great deal of job satisfaction in knowing we are doing the Lord's will, especially when our work for him bears fruit. That is a wonderful reward in itself. And the opposite is true. Every Christian knows the heartache resulting from failure to do something that was clearly our responsibility. Hopefully, we also know the Lord's loving restoration and renewal following such a failure.

On a corporate level there is much to be gained by accountability and reward. If a plan, project or campaign has been successful then the whole church should share in the blessing and it may be of help to others further afield. When there has been a failure we need to be prepared to recognise our mistakes, to learn from them, and to strengthen those who may feel despondent and may need evidence of God's love in a special way.

The Church has shied away from giving material recognition or reward to its successful members as would happen in a secular situation. Christians have recognised that they are God's servants and that 'we have only done our duty' (Luke 17: 10). Christians have been satisfied with the promise of Jesus:

'In my Father's house are many rooms; if it were not so, I would have told you. I am going there to prepare a place for you. And if I go to prepare a place for you, I will come back and take you to be with me that you also may be where I am.' **John 14: 2 & 3**

CHAPTER 14
The final analysis

At the end of the age God is going to re-create the earth - indeed he will create a new heaven and a new earth for the first heaven and the first earth will pass away (Revelation 21: 1). Perhaps the re-creation is necessary because of the mess we have made of this planet. We have killed off many species of birds, animals, insects and plants and by pollution and exploitation have upset the balance of nature.

The nations of the world are not evolving into a super society where social ills have been eradicated. War, violence, oppression, crime, child abuse and even slavery - all are still with us in various forms and the wealthiest of nations have not found lasting answers. Indeed, they often face an escalation in violence and crime. There is a decline in moral standards as man turns his back on God and opts for a situational ethic.

The arrival of the Messiah held out hope for humanity for 'in him was life, and that life was the light of men'. But 'the light shines in the darkness, [but] the darkness has not understood it' (John 1: 4, 5). In spite of all the efforts of the Church down the centuries, the world, like a pendulum, swings back and forth it moves towards accepting and then rejecting the Law of God.

In the final analysis in God's re-creation

> the dwelling of God [will be] with men, and he will live with them. They will be his people, and God himself will be with them and be their God. He will wipe every tear from their eyes. There will be no more death or mourning or crying or pain, for the old order of things has passed away. **Revelation 21: 3, 4**

One day God will put right the wrongs of this world but in the meantime we should press on to our high calling of being the light of the world and the salt of the earth until on that day of final reckoning each one of us, as stewards has to give account to Almighty God.

It does not help to ignore the hard sayings of Jesus and so as we consider the matter of accountability and reward we return to the Parable of the Talents that we considered in Chapter 2. The first two stewards have doubled their master's investment and received their reward but the third went and hid the talent he was given in the ground. The master's response is not easy to understand:

'Take the talent from him and give it to the one who has the ten talents. For everyone who has will be given more, and he will have an abundance. Whoever does not have, even what he has will be taken from him. And throw that worthless servant outside, into the darkness, where there will be weeping and gnashing of teeth.' **Matthew 25: 28 - 30**

This is not an isolated response, taken out of context; for Jesus went on to speak of the sheep and the goats.

'Then the King will say to those on his right, "Come, you who are blessed by my Father; take your inheritance, the kingdom prepared for you since the creation of the world..."

Then he will say to those on his left, "Depart from me, you who are cursed, into the eternal fire prepared for the devil and his angels. "' **Matthew 25: 34, 41**

Accountability and reward are part of the Gospel. We cannot ignore them. But anyone who has tasted and seen that the Lord is good, who has experienced Calvary love and the renewing of the Holy Spirit; that person responds, not out of fear but out of love.

Adam and Moses were men and we are fellow stewards with them of God's world and God's law. Jesus is God and for a while walked here on earth, fully God and fully man. We are stewards of his Gospel. We are his ambassadors and through him we have a greater responsibility than Adam or Moses but also a greater authority and a new relationship with him and his Father.

> 'I no longer call you servants, because a servant does not know his master's business. Instead, I have called you friends, for everything that I learned from my Father I have made known to you. You did not choose me, but I chose you to go and bear fruit - fruit that will last. ... Greater love has no one than this, that one lay down his life for his friends. You are my friends if you do what I command. This is my command: Love each other.'
> **John 15: 14 - 17**, order slightly rearranged.

I believe Mother Theresa had a method of daily accountability that involves two prayers, each of five words. In the morning she reminded herself that:

He did it for me!

In the evening she asked herself:

I did what for Him?

That is the steward's prayer.

CHAPTER 15

The Christian Steward: RICH TOWARD GOD

We end where we started. The title of the book is the title of this chapter – The Christian Steward: Rich toward God.

The title page of the book gives two verses of a parable the NIV calls 'The Parable of the Rich Fool'. We must now consider the parable.

> Someone in the crowd said to him, 'Teacher, tell my brother to divide the inheritance with me.'
>
> Jesus replied, 'Man, who appointed me a judge or an arbiter between you?' Then he said to them, 'Watch out! Be on your guard against all kinds of greed; a man's life does not consist in the abundance of his possessions.'
>
> And he told them this parable: 'The ground of a certain rich man produced a good crop. He thought to himself, "What shall I do? I have no place to store my crops."
>
> 'Then he said, "This is what I'll do. I will tear down my barns and build bigger ones, and there I will store all my grain and my goods. And I'll say to myself, "You have plenty of good things laid up for many years. Take life easy; eat, drink and be merry."'
>
> But God said to him, "You fool! This very night your life will be demanded from you. Then who will get what you have prepared for yourself?"
>
> 'This is how it will be with anyone who stores up things for himself but is not rich toward God.' **Luke 12: 13 - 21**

The Lord Jesus used a request from the crowd to introduce one of the most challenging messages of his ministry.

Two brothers were squabbling over their inheritance. The one wanted Jesus to intervene. Jesus refused to be drawn into their personal battle but did point to the root cause of their problem. Their problem is our problem. It is the age-old problem: greed. The proverbial coin has two sides; one is greed, the other is covetousness. We start by coveting and end up greedy. We don't just covet what our neighbour has; we want more than he has.

Greed sums up the philosophy of a world without Christ - and sadly sometimes even of those who know him. Greed is a god who is never satisfied. He makes great promises but his followers are after the pot of gold at the end of the rainbow. We want more, we want newer, we want bigger, we want better. We are never content.

Greed is a pervasive cancer. It takes many forms, one of the commonest being the 'love of money', the root of all kinds of evil. The advertising gurus of our age exploit our greed in all its forms in trying to persuade us that we 'need' the latest product because we will look better, look affluent, feel good, and enjoy the attention we deserve. We pay ludicrous prices for products of dubious effectiveness. Beware of advertising. For advertising is so successful that in the face of strong medical evidence that smoking causes cancer many people are still prepared to take up this expensive and deadly habit.

Jesus contradicts the wisdom of this and every age, 'a man's life does *not* consist in the abundance of his possessions'.

He illustrated his point by telling a parable. There is a rich man. His fields produce a bumper crop. The rain came at the right time and in the right amount. The sun shone when it was needed. He has more than ever before. So much so that his barns are too small. He decides to do what any industrious person would do; he will build bigger barns to store the grain. Then he will be able to live off the accumulated wealth. He will stop working and take early retirement. He will fulfil his dream, a life of ease with the sole purpose of enjoying himself. Bliss!

Does the dream sound familiar? Isn't it a reasonable dream?

After all, we have worked hard for many years. Surely we are entitled to enjoy the fruit of our labour? (Does this sound like the advertisement for a pension scheme or an exotic holiday?)

This rich man had made one fundamental error.

He had thought only of himself. Not once does he show any interest in the welfare of others. By human standards the rich man had been very wise in preparing for the future - he would even be commended for astute forward planning - a wise man indeed.

But God calls him a fool!

Why does God call him a fool? Because the rich man is preparing for a future over which he has no control. God is taking it away 'this very night'. And all the man's hard work is futile as he will not be able to enjoy it himself.

The next verse reveals that the Lord Jesus knew the heart of God, for he adds a new dimension to an existing teaching. The wisdom of the Old Testament was that 'He who is kind to the poor lends to the Lord, and he will reward him for what he has done' (Proverbs 19: 17). It is an interesting concept. What we give to the poor is a loan to God, a loan that he will repay. But the amazing difference that Jesus makes clear in our title verse is that God expects us to be rich in giving to him.

We are to be rich toward God. We, who are so used to receiving from our heavenly Father, can actually be generous in giving to him. He deems our offerings as his personal gifts. We are in a new personal relationship with our heavenly Father; we are his children. He gives us gifts and we give him gifts.

Every parent treasures a gift from a child. The gift may have cost little in money but much in love. We love to receive them. So does our Father. God loves our gifts. In giving to the church or a missionary organisation or for relief work we are giving to God. God has not been miserly in his gifts to us - we should not be miserly in our gifts to him. He has given us the riches of his grace and because of that grace we are able to give richly to our God.

According to the headings in the NIV Bible the parable of the rich fool ends with verse 21. This is misleading as the story continues through two more headings: 'Do Not Worry' and 'Watchfulness'. Both are very important to our theme as the Lord used the parable as an opportunity for teaching on the right way to view money and wealth. He moved on to teach the disciples about the need to be prepared for his return.

As both sections are important they are given in full. The opening words of verse 22 indicate that they follow on from verse 21.

Do Not Worry

Then Jesus said to his disciples: 'Therefore I tell you, do not worry about your life, what you will eat; or about your body, what you will wear. Life is more than food, and the body more than clothes. Consider the ravens: They do not sow or reap, they have no storeroom or barn; yet God feeds them. And how much more valuable you are than birds! Who of you by worrying can add a single hour to his life? Since you cannot do this very little thing, why do you worry about the rest?

'Consider how the lilies grow. They do not labour or spin. Yet I tell you, not even Solomon in all his splendour was dressed like one of these. If that is how God clothes the grass of the field, which is here today, and tomorrow is thrown into the fire, how much more will he clothe you, O you of little faith! And do not set your heart on what you will eat or drink; do not worry about it. For the pagan world runs after all such things, and your Father knows that you need them. But seek his kingdom, and these things will be given to you as well.

'Do not be afraid, little flock, for your Father has been pleased to give you the kingdom. Sell your possessions and give to the poor. Provide purses for yourselves that will not wear out, a treasure in heaven that will not be exhausted, where no thief comes near and no moth destroys. For where your treasure is, there your heart will be also. **Luke 12: 22 - 34**

The Lord tells us that if we are committed to the principle of being rich toward God then we do not need to worry about the material things of life. God will take care of those. Our treasure should be in heaven. If it is not, if it is here on earth, then our hearts will be caught up with earthly things and of very little use to our Father in heaven.

Watchfulness

The next passage takes up the theme of watchfulness.

Be dressed ready for service and keep your lamps burning, like men waiting for their master to return from a wedding banquet, so that when he comes and knocks they can immediately open the door for him. It will be good for those servants whose master finds them watching when he comes. I tell you the truth, he will dress himself to serve, will have them recline at the table and will come and wait on them. It will be good for those servants whose master finds them ready, even if he comes in the second or third watch of the night. But understand this: If the owner of the house had known at what hour the thief was coming, he would not have let his house be broken into. You also must be ready, because the Son of Man will come at an hour when you do not expect him.

Peter asked, 'Lord, are you telling this parable to us, or to everyone?

The Lord answered, 'Who then is the faithful and wise manager, whom the master puts in charge of his servants to give them their food allowance at the proper time? It will be good for that servant whom the master finds doing so when he returns. I tell you the truth, he will put him in charge of all his possessions. But suppose the servant says to himself, 'My master is taking a long time in coming,' and he then begins to beat the menservants and womenservants and to eat and drink and get drunk. The master of that servant will come on a day when he does not expect him and at an hour he is not aware of. He will cut him to pieces and assign him a place with the unbelievers.

That servant who knows his master's will and does not get ready or does not do what his master wants will be beaten with many blows. But the one who does not know and does things deserving punishment will be beaten with few blows. From everyone who has been given much, much will be demanded; and from the one who has been entrusted with much, much more will be asked. **Luke 12: 35 – 48**

Being a steward is a fulltime, lifetime commitment to serve the Master. To be ready all the time in case he returns and calls us to give an account. For those who are eagerly waiting his return, the Lord Jesus says that he will change his royal robes and put on a servant's clothing. Why? So that he can wait on us at the great feast which will be our reception in the place that he has gone ahead to prepare for us. That is the joy of the master!

Peter asked if the parable was limited in its application. The Lord's reply is that it applies to all stewards. The servant who knows his master's will be judged more severely than the ignorant servant but ignorance is not an excuse. What is more there is no point in being envious of another's gifts as more is expected of someone gifted.

Let me remind you again of Paul's words to timid Timothy,

Command those who are rich in this present world not to be arrogant nor to put their hope in wealth, which is so uncertain, but to put their hope in God, who richly provides us with everything for our enjoyment. Command them to do good, to be rich in good deeds, and to be generous and willing to share. In this way they will lay up treasure for themselves as a firm foundation for the coming age, so that they may take hold of the life that is truly life. **1 Timothy 6: 17 – 19**

The contrast in the passage is between 'this present world' and 'the coming age'. The former will pass away, the latter is truly life. The present lasts but a lifetime, the future is for all eternity.

Now is the time to be rich toward God.

Bibliography

Randy Alcorn – *Money, Possessions and Eternity* (Wheaton, Il: Tyndale House Publishers, 1989)

Jacinta Ashworth & Ian Farthing – *Churchgoing in the UK* (London: Tearfund, 2007)

Barclay, W - *Ethics in a Permissive Society* (Fontana, 1971)

Ken Burnett – *Relationship Fundraising* (London, The White Lion Press Ltd, 192)

Ash Carter – *The Money Mentor* (Nottingham, UK: Inter-Varsity Press, 2010 edition)

Sir Fred Catherwood – *God's Time God's Money* (Sevenoaks, UK: Hodder & Stoughton, 1998)

Ian Coffey – *Pennies for Heaven* (Eastbourne, UK: Kingsway Publications, 1984 edition)

Everald Compton – *Living with Money* (Auckland, NZ: Hodder & Stoughton, 1983 edition)

Everald Compton – *Where Have The Christian Stewards Gone?* (Ilfracombe, Devon: Arthur H Stockwell: 1979 edition)

Howard Dayton – *Your Money Counts* (Wheaton, Il: Tyndale House Publishers, 1997 edition)

Michael Griffiths – *Take my life* (London, UK: Inter-Varsity Press, 1975 edition)

R T Kendall – *The Gift of Giving* (London: Hodder & Stoughton, 1998 edition)

Redina Kolaneci – *Why Christians Give* (Colchester, UK: McConkey Johnston international UK, 2010)

Mark Noblin – *Rich Toward God* (Plano, TX: The Rock Outreach. 2008 edition)

Stephen F Olford – *The Grace of Giving* (London: Lakeland 1972)

John Preston - *Giving for Life* (The Archbishop's Council 2009)

John Preston – *The Money Revolution* (London: Authentic Media, 2007 edition)

R Scott Rodin – *Stewards in the Kingdom* (Downers Grove, Il: Inter-Varsity Press, 2000 edition)

Ronald J Sider – *Rich Christians in an Age of Hunger* (Nashville, USA: Thomas Nelson, 2005 edition)

John Stott – *The Grace of Giving* (London: Langham Partnership International/The Lausanne Movement, 2008 edition)

Tondeur, Keith - *What Price the Lottery?* (Monarch, 1996)

John White – *Money isn't God* (Leicester, UK: Inter-Varsity Press, 1993 edition)

Michael Wright – *Yours, Lord* (London, UK: Mowbray, 1992 edition)

Marshall, M., *The Gospel Connection*, DLT 1991